Succeeding in Your Work and Community

Patricia L. Duffy
T. Walter Wannie

Interior Layout: Wendy Ford

Succeeding in Your Work and Community
©1995 JIST Works, Inc.
720 North Park Avenue
Indianapolis, IN 46202-3431
Phone 317-264-3720   Fax 317-264-3709

99   98   3   4   5   6   7   8   9

Printed in the United States of America.

ISBN: 1-56370-190-1

Books in the Series
Hire Learning, Schooling That Works

Setting Your Career and Life Direction: Helps students set career and life goals and make good decisions regarding careers and education. Also explains why communication skills and getting along with others are essential to job success.

Landing a Job: Covers everything needed to find a good job, including interview skills, getting leads from people you know, networking, following up, resumés, applications, and more.

Succeeding in Your Work and Community: Good advice on keeping a job and getting ahead, exploring self-employment options, changing jobs, making good decisions, and succeeding in the community.

Instructor's Guide: Provides tips for using *Hire Learning* as the basis for a career development course or for infusing it into another class. Includes goals, in-class activities, handouts, home-work suggestions, community activities, and other useful information.

Contents

Foreword

About half of all the new jobs created in the next 10 years will require education or training beyond high school. Most of the fastest-growing and better-paying jobs require technical training or college-level education. But whether or not you decide to get more education after high school, all employers want workers who can communicate effectively, get along well with others, and have a positive attitude toward themselves and their work.

Making the transition from school to work is difficult for most people. One research study found that two-thirds of all adult workers would do things differently after high school if they could plan those years over again. To make this transition easier, start planning now for your career, your education, and your life. Planning now can have important and long-term effects on your future. You can always change your mind later.

About the Authors and This Revision

The *Hire Learning, Schooling That Works* series was originally written and self-published by the authors to bring improved career education materials to high school students. These real-life workplace lessons combine applied academics, life skills, and employability skills in a form that can be infused into existing classes or used as the basis for a separate program or course.

The initial reception to the *Hire Learning* material was universally enthusiastic. Part of the reason for this positive reaction is that the authors were teachers who had many years of classroom and vocational education experience. Another reason for *Hire Learning's* enthusiastic reception was that it had been field-tested. Numerous instructors and thousands of students used earlier versions, and revisions and improvements were based on their suggestions.

Unfortunately, Patricia Duffy died of cancer several years ago, which made further revisions to the *Hire Learning* series impractical. Walter Wannie kept the material available but could not afford to market it professionally or continue updating it. When I first saw the *Hire Learning* material, I was impressed. Walter and I agreed that JIST should revise the material, keeping it within national career development guidelines.

This new edition of the *Hire Learning* curriculum is completely revised, but the original enthusiasm, engaging style, and practical common sense are still very much here. Pat's work lives on through the pages of this and the other books in the *Hire Learning, Schooling That Works* series. We think that Pat would be pleased.

Mike Farr

Mike Farr is president of JIST Works, Inc., and author of *The Very Quick Job Search, The Quick Resumé and Cover Letter Book, America's 50 Fastest Growing Jobs,* and many other job search and career books.

Introduction

elcome to **Hire Learning**, a best-seller you won't want to leave home or school without. Why not? Because **Hire Learning** tells about you!

Hire Learning is your personal career counselor. It shows you how to find, keep, and wisely change jobs and careers, both now and throughout your working life. To make sure that you won't find career education boring, this three-book series focuses on you. Using **Hire Learning** as your guide, you write your own career education — you ask and answer the important questions, you create the assignments. When it's over, you apply what you've learned about yourself every time you want to be HIRED!

Hire Learning puts you in charge of your future — helping you learn about yourself, make choices, review options, and compare what you already know with what you need to learn. It guides you through workbook exercises to classroom projects to one-on-one conversations with parents, friends, workers, and role models. These activities all focus on planning for a future of work you enjoy — work that brings you self-esteem, fulfillment, and dignity.

- In Book 1, *Setting Your Career and Life Direction*, you compile a list of personal interests, talents, and abilities, relating them to fields of work that could put them to good use. You explore your values and life goals so you can make better choices about jobs and careers. You also learn important communication skills for getting along with others, to help you succeed in any work you do.

- In Book 2, *Landing a Job*, you put together your work history and develop an effective resume and cover letter. You learn how to make networking contacts, follow up job leads, fill out job applications, and prepare for job interviews. You practice answering difficult interview questions openly and honestly.

■ In Book 3, *Succeeding in Your Work and Community*, you learn about keeping your job, changing jobs, overcoming barriers, working for yourself, and picking up skills and qualities that will keep you in demand.

You'll come away from your **Hire Learning** experience understanding how your schoolwork counts in the workplace. You'll learn how reading, writing, listening, following directions, and understanding computers can make you a valued employee — or how the lack of such skills can put you out of work.

But even more important, **Hire Learning** starts you on the path of "lifelong learning," a habit of growth and self-awareness that will guide you for years to come. As your responsibilities, values, and behaviors change over time, you'll be able to use this best-seller over and over again. It will be your handy pocket guide to employability.

If you are like most people, you'll spend more than 30 years in the world of work, during which you'll change jobs eight to 10 times and change careers at least three times. You may be the sole provider for yourself and your family. Or, you may share the load with another wage earner. Some of you will choose to work in the corporate world. Others of you will start your own businesses so you can work for yourselves. Whichever path you take, you'll benefit from strengthening your self-understanding and balancing your dreams with reality. **Hire Learning** will help you in that process, right now.

One thing's certain: Never before has learning how to be gainfully employed been more important. You've heard the horror stories about low-paying, part-time, dead-end jobs that don't offer a dependable way to support yourself and your family or to hold your head high. You know about the barriers put up by prejudice and discrimination. In today's job market, you must strive to be the best you can be, or face a grim work life. Without a resolve to learn the skills the workplace demands, you face many years of looking forward to Friday and dreading Monday. You must be willing to learn from others and take responsibility for your own growth.

So put yourself on the "best-seller list" as you read and grow with **Hire Learning**. Study the books carefully and do the exercises. Discuss what you discover with family, friends, counselors, and instructors. Ask for their opinions and suggestions. Talk with workers of every age, color, sex, and job description in your neighborhood and city. Learn from the experiences these people can share with you. Learn all you can about the career fields you're interested in.

Most of all, learn to "sell yourself" with pride, productivity, and performance. That's what **Hire Learning** is all about.

Patricia L. Duffy
T. Walter Wannie

Starting
Out
Right

hen you step into the world of work, believe in your **Hire Learning**. With determination, initiative, and a serious commitment to your education, YOU can positively change the workplace of the future. Your example can inspire those around you, whether you work in a small business, large corporation, factory, office, laboratory, hospital, or production center.

How will others recognize your **Hire Learning**? First, you will appreciate the value of schooling and of lifelong learning. Second, you will use your personal "work history" to strengthen your employability potential. Third, you will show your ability to communicate with employers, co-workers, and everyone you meet.

Most important, your self-knowledge and dedication to lifelong learning will empower you. You will plan your career skillfully. You will be living proof that the workplace can be improved by the strength and will of the workers. Because of your work ethic, talents, abilities, aptitudes, and values, those who follow your path will regard you as a mentor and role model.

In this section, we look at what employers will expect of you on the job, and how you can put your **Hire Learning** to work in the workplace.

Employability Tips

What makes you a good employee? Why would the person who hired you want to keep you employed? Here are some tips for making a strong showing in the workplace.

✓ Start smart.

Just as you should begin a new school year or course of study with a positive attitude and a desire to learn, you should approach employability skills with the same type of "mental fitness." When applying for a job, you've got one goal — getting hired.

You'll feel proud that an employer has chosen you from among other applicants and that your skills, behaviors, and attitudes are recognized for their value to a company. Getting off to a good start means that you want to prove to yourself and others that you are deserving of this honor.

✓ Show up on time.

Students who are never late never miss any of the learning process that happens in class. Students who are punctual also get a reputation for responsibility, hard work, and dependability — qualities that will be lead to success later in life.

When you begin your first job, know when and where you are to report to start your new duties. Arrange for transportation and prepare to take care of any problem that could make you late. No one at the work site is there to give you extra time or set the alarm for you. You alone are in charge of your actions. Make sure you are ready to adopt this adult behavior.

✓ Be worker fit.

Head-to-toe fitness seems to be everyone's goal these days. But what about worker fitness? Can you make the delicate machine of the human body and mind be "worker fit"? You can if you use common sense and good judgment in your work life.

Your instructors remind you the night before exams to get a good night's rest and to eat sensibly. That gives you a fueled mind and body, ready to take on new challenges. When beginning a new job, the same guideline applies. New situations take extra fuel. They put stress on the mind and body, which can make you tired. If you want to be "worker fit," live a healthy lifestyle at home so you can be your best at work.

✓ Be serious.

Nothing is more disturbing to an employer than a worker with a careless, frivolous attitude. Maturity is always favored over silliness. Sometimes nervousness in a new situation can make you act overly familiar with others or act silly to get attention. But that kind of behavior won't win you "Employee of the Month" awards!

Self-control is one of the most important employability skills. Today's workplace is filled with pressures, deadlines, and demands. If you remain calm in pressured times, cope with unexpected emergencies, and deliver quality work with pride, you show that you are a mature, serious-minded adult.

✓ Follow the rules.

There are rules, rights, and responsibilities in any workplace. Most beginning workers are given an Employee Handbook that lists these rules and rights. Some workers take part in new employee seminars and special training programs. Others are expected to blend in almost immediately and follow loosely defined guidelines. No matter in what situation you find yourself, remember: Rules are meant to be followed.

If you've done your homework about your job or work site, you will already know the dress code, the time work starts and ends, and other rules and expectations before your first day. Take all rules seriously.

✓ Be willing to learn.

No one comes to a job with every skill needed to perform the tasks perfectly. Everyone can learn new things and learn from others. One of the best characteristics of a worker is a willingness to listen and learn. Sometimes skills are routine, but sometimes skills are learned from watching and imitating others. Even if you have done the same job in a different workplace, you are now employed by someone else, and you need to do things the way your new employer wants them done.

Does this mean that you will never be allowed to offer ideas of your own? Does it mean that you have to throw your imagination and creativity out the window and conform? Of course not. But the opportunity to be an innovator and offer ideas comes only after you've been in a job for awhile and built a

good reputation. You don't decide to run the company after the first day on the job. Offer ideas for change slowly, and only to your direct supervisor.

✓ Ask questions.

A person who is willing to learn asks questions. But think carefully first. Don't ask questions that, with a little thought, you could have answered for yourself. Knowing when to ask questions is a matter of experience and judgment.

Make sure you do ask when you really don't understand something. Nothing is worse than pretending you understand something when you don't, and then making mistakes because of it. Take notes of answers you get, so you can review them later. A new employee is expected to need extra information, so don't be embarrassed if you don't understand all the procedures and routines right away.

✓ Communicate well with others.

This is a big responsibility. You may be in a work situation where some of your coworkers don't even speak your language. You may have to work side-by-side with bullies, braggers, and gossips. Situations like these may be difficult and may put your interpersonal skills to the test.

Some general guidelines will help you: Believe in yourself and recognize that positive feelings you have about yourself can be transferred to others. Think of times when you have felt proud because of a compliment or because you did something good for someone. Now transfer these same feelings to those you work with. Practice positive manners. Look others straight in the eye when talking or listening. Be courteous. Be impressed by their accomplishments, rather than jealous. Be friendly, but always with reserve. Make sure that you don't develop an exclusive group of friends — a clique — and shut out others. You will enjoy some people's company more than others', but be open to everyone.

✓ Behave ethically.

It's an age of business scandals, environmental scams, phony resumes, and other acts of unethical behavior. An employer appreciates a worker who is honest, trustworthy, and loyal, and who practices good judgment when tempted to cut corners, spread rumors, misuse property, or commit a dishonest act.

Ethical behavior is deeply rooted in your values. **Hire Learning** has included many exercises to help you identify, clarify, and act on your values so that when you enter the world of work you will act with integrity.

✓ Create a business image.

Appropriate clothing and good grooming are only part of creating a winning business image. Equally important is how you stand, move, and talk.

A strong image shows up in a smile, an energetic step, a posture of mental alertness, and enthusiastic conversation. You've probably never seen an advertisement in which a successful executive appears leaning on his or her elbows, looking lazy, dejected, or frazzled.

That doesn't mean that you'll never feel stress at work. But if foot-dragging and unhappy expressions are part of your image, you're hurting your chances for success. That image suggests that you don't care about work or yourself, or that you're in poor health, or that you're just bored. Such an image lowers worker productivity, which leads to getting fired!

✓ **Be proud to work with others who accomplish.**

Nothing tears down the fabric of the workplace more than workers who are jealous of their coworkers. Workplaces today are built around group decisions, consensus, and teamwork. This setting requires workers who work to the best of their ability and offer that talent and skill to others. Applauding the accomplishments of others shows maturity, makes others feel valued, and improves the productivity and efficiency of the team. Every person likes to be recognized. Be a worker who shows self-respect by respecting others.

✓ **Avoid radical ideas and behaviors.**

Wild, way-out actions usually bother employers. Even if some workers do wild things to make a point or promote an important cause, employers prefer that they work conservatively within the system to create change. Union membership, political ideologies, and other confrontational issues need to be addressed with mature judgment.

✓ **Be honest.**

Never lie — it will come back to haunt you. Suppose you have been convicted of a crime, and yet you lie about that on your job application. Employers can check such information easily. You'll be caught in a lie, and after that, you'll have no credibility — no one will trust you. Making up stories about your previous employers and work situations is another example of dishonest behavior. Don't lie about your age, the reasons you were fired, grades . . . don't lie about anything!

✓ **Respect yourself.**

You have the power within yourself to be the best you can be. Be proud of who you are, your skills, talents, abilities, education, and heritage. Compete only with yourself, because your performance review is yours alone. If you are doing a good job, your efforts will be praised and recognized. If you need more direction, supervision, or training, believe that this help is in your best interest, and follow through with integrity. In that way, your learning power and self-respect will be challenged. You will be well on your way to meeting your needs through **Hire Learning.**

Priorities That Count

Your employer *chooses* to hire you, so you need to know what is important to your employer. Make sure you deliver that. In other words, make your employer's priorities your priorities.

This exercise tests your sense of what employers expect from workers. How would an employer react the first time a worker made a certain mistake?

Read each "worker error," and predict how strongly an employer would react to that error by checking one response from *ignore it* to *fire the worker.* Base your choices on the kinds of jobs you are likely to have, work you have already done, or information learned in your school-to-work transition lessons.

WORKER ERROR   EMPLOYER RESPONSE

What would most employers do the first time a worker...	*Ignore It*	*Discuss It, If It Continues*	*Discuss It Right Away*	*Warn the Worker*	*Suspend the Worker*	*Fire the Worker*
1. Didn't call in when sick?	___	___	___	___	___	___
2. Refused to do a job because it was undesirable or demeaning?	___	___	___	___	___	___
3. Missed two days of work the first month?	___	___	___	___	___	___
4. Seemed not to be trying, but was just as productive as other workers?	___	___	___	___	___	___
5. Needed twice as much supervision as others?	___	___	___	___	___	___
6. Spoke so poorly that coworkers couldn't understand what was being said?	___	___	___	___	___	___

WORKER ERROR	EMPLOYER RESPONSE					
What would most employers do the first time a worker...	*Ignore It*	*Discuss It, If It Continues*	*Discuss It Right Away*	*Warn the Worker*	*Suspend the Worker*	*Fire the Worker*
7. Griped about working conditions such as short coffee breaks or having to work an unpopular shift?	____	____	____	____	____	____
8. Didn't try and was 15% less productive than other workers who had the same training?	____	____	____	____	____	____
9. Came to work dirty or sloppy?	____	____	____	____	____	____
10. Wore flashy or sexy clothes to work?	____	____	____	____	____	____
11. Finished assigned work but didn't report back to the boss for more work?	____	____	____	____	____	____
12. Took an additional hour of break time but finished assigned work anyway?	____	____	____	____	____	____
13. Showed up for work drunk or high on drugs?	____	____	____	____	____	____
14. Acted angry or sulked when criticized?	____	____	____	____	____	____
15. Made many mistakes adding, subtracting, multiplying, or dividing numbers?	____	____	____	____	____	____
16. Caused $100 damage to a piece of equipment?	____	____	____	____	____	____
17. Was 20 minutes late for work and had no good excuse?	____	____	____	____	____	____
18. Couldn't read written directions to complete a job?	____	____	____	____	____	____

©1995 JIST Works, Inc.

9

WORKER ERROR	EMPLOYER RESPONSE					
What would most employers do the first time a worker...	*Ignore It*	*Discuss It, If It Continues*	*Discuss It Right Away*	*Warn the Worker*	*Suspend the Worker*	*Fire the Worker*
19. Tried, but took twice as long as other workers to learn a new job?	_____	_____	_____	_____	_____	_____
20. Wrote phone messages or memos that were impossible to read?	_____	_____	_____	_____	_____	_____
21. Made many mistakes in spelling, grammar, and punctuation?	_____	_____	_____	_____	_____	_____
22. Tried, but was 15% less productive than other workers who had the same training?	_____	_____	_____	_____	_____	_____
23. Put more hours on the time sheet than actually worked?	_____	_____	_____	_____	_____	_____
24. Got into an argument with coworkers?	_____	_____	_____	_____	_____	_____
25. Spent 15 minutes making personal phone calls during one work day?	_____	_____	_____	_____	_____	_____

Source: National Center for Research in Vocational Education, *The Employer's Choice: Resource Manual* (Columbus, Ohio: Center on Education and Training for Employment [formerly NCRVE], Ohio State University). Copyright 1987. Used with permission.

Working Words

N ow that you are learning about the world of work — and listening to people talk about it — you'll hear new job-related words. From time to time, you will fill out forms and answer questions that use a "work" vocabulary. You'll have to understand these words used by bosses and coworkers so you can respond in a way that's positive and gets your points across.

Test your work vocabulary skills by matching each word or phrase below to its definition. Write the definition's number next to the word in the space provided. The first one is already done to help you get started.

Words to Define

__59__ Access	_____ Fringe Benefits
_____ Affirmative Action	_____ Grievance
_____ Apprentice	_____ Grievance Procedure
_____ Aptitude	_____ Harassment
_____ Bonus	_____ Hazard
_____ Break Time	_____ Health & Insurance Plan
_____ Collective Bargaining	_____ Job Action
_____ Commission Earnings	_____ Job Description
_____ Continuing Education	_____ Job Posting
_____ Cost-of-Living Adjustment (COLA)	_____ Job Sharing
_____ Disability Retirement	_____ Layoff (Workforce Reduction)
_____ Discharge	_____ Leave
_____ Discrimination	_____ Maternity Benefits
_____ Docked	_____ Mentor
_____ Equal Opportunity Employer	_____ Merger
_____ FICA (Fed. Insurance Contributions Act)	_____ Merit Increase
_____ Flex Time	_____ Minimum Wage

Words to Define *cont'd*

_____ Moonlighting	_____ Shift
_____ On-the-Job Training	_____ Social Security Act
_____ Overtime	_____ Specialist
_____ Paid Holidays	_____ Strike
_____ Payroll Deductions	_____ Take-Home Pay
_____ Picketers	_____ Time Clock
_____ Probationary Period	_____ Time and a Half
_____ Profit-Sharing Plan	_____ Trait
_____ Punch Card	_____ Unemployment Insurance
_____ Qualifications	_____ Withholding Tax
_____ Resume	_____ Workers' Compensation
_____ Retirement	_____ Work-to-Rule
_____ Seniority	_____ Work Record

Definitions

(1) Any payment in addition to regular pay

(2) A joint federal/state program under which unemployed people are paid for a limited period of time

(3) Unequal treatment of workers in hiring, employment, pay, or work conditions because of race, national origin, creed, color, sex, age, union membership or activity, or any other characteristics not related to ability or job performance

(4) A natural ability to learn or develop a certain skill

(5) A quality or characteristic

(6) A federal law governing the social security taxes that most workers have to pay

(7) A record of all the places a person has worked and information about work performance

(8) Action taken when money is deducted from a worker's pay, usually as a penalty for being late for work

(9) The hours a person works that exceed the regular work week or schedule; also the pay a worker receives for those extra hours, which are often paid at one and one-half ("time and a half") or two times the regular pay rate

(10) A brief interruption during work, often five to 15 minutes long, when workers can rest or take refreshments without losing pay

(11) Negotiations between representatives of the employees and the employer to determine the conditions of employment, usually resulting in a written contract that spells out the wages and other conditions until the next bargaining session

(12) Retirement because of physical inability to perform the job

(13) A person who works for another for a set term to learn job skills

(14) A person who devotes him or herself to one job or career

(15) Learning job skills while being employed

(16) A brief listing of personal, educational, and professional qualifications for a job

(17) The lowest hourly pay rate workers can be paid, by law

(18) Money regularly taken out of a person's paycheck for taxes, dues, benefits, and other purposes

(19) To fire a worker

(20) A formal complaint or expression of dissatisfaction made by an employee about job conditions, pay, or other aspects of employment

(21) The skills and experience required to do a job

(22) Raising or lowering wages or salaries to match changes in the cost of living, as determined by the Consumer Price Index

Definitions *cont'd*

(23) Earnings for a payroll period minus the deductions (such as taxes); the actual amount of cash a worker ends up with

(24) A program, paid for in whole or in part by the employer, that provides money to help the worker and his or her family in case of death, illness, accidents, and other events

(25) A written statement that lists the duties of a particular job

(26) A machine that accurately prints or punches the time on a worker's "punch card" to record when the worker starts and stops work

(27) Benefits, like insurance or paid vacation, which a worker gets in addition to salary

(28) A special card that a worker inserts in a time clock to record the time he or she starts and leaves work

(29) Income taxes automatically taken out of an employee's paycheck and paid to the government

(30) A listing of available jobs in the company so employees may bid for promotions or transfers

(31) Removing a worker from a job and stopping pay, temporarily or permanently, not because the worker did anything wrong, but because business is slow or a company is changing and doesn't need the worker

(32) A pay increase given to reward performance

(33) Special health benefits and time off for workers (and sometimes workers' wives) during pregnancy and after childbirth

(34) Allowable time away from work for sickness, vacations, personal time, or other reasons (paid or unpaid)

(35) Holding more than one paid job at a time

(36) Days of special religious, cultural, social, or patriotic importance on which workers get paid without working

(37) A scheduled segment of the daily work schedule of a plant or its employees; a factory that runs 24 hours a day usually has three eight-hour shifts a day

(38) A system of insurance required by law that pays workers or their families when a worker gets hurt or sick while on the job and can't earn a living for a period

(39) A federal insurance program that provides, among other benefits, retirement income, disability payments, and public assistance to the aged, blind, and needy

(40) A specified period, such as 30 days, during which a newly hired employee is being "tried out" before the company commits to keeping the worker permanently and before benefits take effect

(41) A temporary stopping of work by a group of employees to express a grievance, enforce a demand for changes in job conditions, or resolve a dispute with management

Definitions *cont'd*

(42) An agreement in which the employer pays employees a share of the profits in addition to their regular pay to motivate them

(43) Leaving working life because of age, disability, financial independence, or other reasons

(44) Special money paid to salespeople based on how much they sell; usually a percentage of the dollars they bring in through sales

(45) A formal set of steps for handling employee grievances

(46) A system for making sure the company's hiring practices don't exclude minority workers

(47) Undergoing school or special training to improve job skills even after being hired

(48) An employer who is dedicated to providing an environment free from discrimination in hiring, promotions, transfers, employee relations, etc.

(49) An agreement whereby employees can work whichever days or hours they please, as long as they complete a certain number of hours per week or complete certain tasks on schedule

(50) Persistent disturbance, pestering, or persecution, especially sexual pressure or intimidation

(51) A potential health risk found in a given task or workplace

(52) When two or more employees share one full-time position, splitting hours and responsibilities between them

(53) When workers slow down on purpose to express a grievance; similar to a strike except that workers may keep working

(54) Someone who teaches and advises about career choices

(55) When two or more companies are combined into one company

(56) People who march in front of a company to demonstrate or to discourage others from entering the company during a strike or job action

(57) Privileges and/or job security a worker gets by staying in a job or company for a length of time

(58) Pay for overtime work equal to one and one-half times the regular hourly wage

(59) Facilities for entering a workplace and using its equipment; federal law requires that companies ensure that proper access is provided for disabled workers in the form of curb ramps, elevators, and other facilities

(60) An agreement under which union members cannot be expected to perform any task that exceeds the minimum requirements in their job descriptions

Answers

(59) Access	(54) Mentor
(46) Affirmative Action	(55) Merger
(13) Apprentice	(32) Merit Increase
(4) Aptitude	(17) Minimum Wage
(1) Bonus	(35) Moonlighting
(10) Break time	(15) On-the-Job Training
(11) Collective Bargaining	(9) Overtime
(44) Commission Earnings	(36) Paid Holidays
(47) Continuing Education	(18) Payroll Deductions
(22) Cost-of-Living Adjustment	(56) Picketers
(12) Disability Retirement	(40) Probationary Period
(19) Discharge	(42) Profit-Sharing Plan
(3) Discrimination	(28) Punch Card
(8) Docked	(21) Qualifications
(48) Equal Opportunity Employer	(16) Resume
(6) FICA (Federal Insurance Contributions Act)	(43) Retirement
(49) Flex Time	(57) Seniority
(27) Fringe Benefits	(37) Shift
(20) Grievance	(39) Social Security Act
(45) Grievance Procedure	(14) Specialist
(50) Harassment	(41) Strike
(51) Hazard	(23) Take-Home Pay
(24) Health & Insurance Plan	(26) Time Clock
(53) Job Action	(58) Time and a Half
(25) Job Description	(5) Trait
(30) Job Posting	(2) Unemployment Insurance
(52) Job Sharing	(29) Withholding Tax
(31) Layoff (Workforce Reduction)	(38) Workers' Compensation
(34) Leave	(60) Work-to-Rule
(33) Maternity Benefits	(7) Work Record

Overcoming Stereotypes

Over the years, increased attention has been given to issues of equity in the workplace. Title VII of the 1964 Civil Rights Act, the Equal Pay Act of 1963, the Americans with Disabilities Act of 1990, the Equal Employment Opportunity Commission, and affirmative action are examples of efforts to address hiring biases, inequality in wages, and discrimination in the workplace. Employment and advancement should be open to all, without regard for race, ethnicity, national origin, religion, gender, age, or disability.

This section of **Hire Learning** focuses on career opportunities for women. Since gender should not have anything to do with employment, helping people of both sexes understand the career goals of women is a positive step toward overcoming the barriers that have slowed women's progress in the workplace.

Women as Winners

nglish short story writer Katherine Mansfield (1888-1923) wrote: "I want, by understanding myself, to understand others. I want to be all that I am capable of becoming." These words capture the optimistic vision for women of today and tomorrow.

Today women have a chance to break down stereotypes that surrounded their former roles. They have opportunities to:

- Work in careers that are personally satisfying and rewarding.
- Blend personal interests and abilities with career and lifestyle goals.
- Balance family, parenting, and homemaker roles with career and work choices.
- Participate in important community activities.
- Pursue education that enhances their career and lifestyle choices.
- Choose careers that once were deemed "inappropriate" for females.

It was not always so. Among the many myths that go along with a woman's traditional role in society are:

- A woman's place is in the home.
- Women should not take jobs away from men by entering the work force.
- Women are not physically or mentally equipped to perform many work tasks.
- Women choose work as an extra thing to do, not because they want to pursue their own career goals.
- Women don't have to be concerned about work because they almost always end up getting married and being supported by husbands.
- Women go to college only to find a husband.
- Women are intellectually inferior to men in certain subjects, such as math, science, and politics.
- Women simply don't belong in some occupations: President of the United States, the military, the clergy.
- Women who are blonde, slim, and pretty are dumb and silly.
- Women are incapable of owning and operating their own businesses because they lack money sense.

Hundreds of examples prove these myths wrong. Still, biases and barriers against women persist. Only by educating everyone about women's true abilities can these myths be overcome.

Daring to Be Different

A Hall of Fame is filled with exhibits about winners, people who by their talents, skills, abilities, and actions rose above others to excel. More often than not, the winners faced stress, misunderstanding, ridicule, and other roadblocks along the way. Still they made it — they "dared to be different." Here are some examples.

Visionaries dare to be different: Shirley Chisholm, the first African American woman elected to Congress; Amelia Earhart, first woman to fly across the Atlantic; Dr. Mathilde Krim, godmother of AIDS research, fundraising, and awareness; and Maria Mitchell, who sighted a new comet.

Athletes dare to be different by breaking records and winning medals: Wilma Rudolph (track), Babe Didrickson Zaharias (track and golf), Nancy Lopez (golf), Martina Navritalova (tennis), Jackie Joyner-Kersee (track), and Kristi Yamaguchi (figure skating).

Students dare to be different when, despite physical handicaps, they continue to learn and inspire others: Helen Keller, who taught and wrote despite being blind and deaf.

People dare to be different when they stand up for their own rights and the rights of others against odds of sexism and racism: Civil rights protestor Rosa Parks, feminist

Susan B. Anthony, singer Lena Horne, poet Maya Angelou, and novelist Alice Walker.

Scientists dare to be different when they seek new cures, explore new frontiers, and perfect new procedures in spite of adversity: environmentalist Rachel Carson, and astronaut Sally Ride.

Social activists dare to be different when they stand up for their beliefs against all odds: feminists Lucretia Mott and Gloria Steinem; and civil rights activists Coretta Scott King and Indira Ghandi.

Kids dare to be different when they resist the temptations of drugs, alcohol, and peer pressure. The list goes on and on. Each name on it offers an optimistic vision for the future.

When you read about the lives of famous people, you almost always find references to their role models. Ask teachers or coaches why they entered their profession, and many will speak about a certain instructor who cared in that special way, and inspired them. Everyone admires heroes. They inspire us to learn what made them special, so that we might strive for the same qualities ourselves.

Following are some examples of important role models who are women — a list of "female firsts." You may want to expand the list with your own heroines.

Women Who Dared to Be Different

Deborah Sampson	First woman soldier in U.S. Army, 1782	Wore men's clothing to enlist in Continental Army
Maria Mitchell	Astronomer, 1847	Sighted a new comet
Antoinette Brown	First woman ordained minister, 1853	Ministered to First Congregational Church in Butler, New York
Dr. Emeline Roberts Jones	First woman dentist, 1855	Specialized in treating women and children
Dr. Mary Harris Thompson	First woman surgeon, 1863	Specialized in abdominal and pelvic surgery in Chicago
Susan Seward	First African American woman physician, 1870	New York Medical College for Women
Frances E. Willard	First woman college president, 1871	Evanston College for Ladies, Illinois
Charlotte E. Ray	First African American woman lawyer, 1872	Graduated from Howard University
Victoria Claflin Woodhull	First woman presidential candidate, 1872	Founded Radical Reformers Party that nominated her
Margaret Abbott Ethelda Bleibtrey Aileen Riggins Tenley Albright Wilma Rudolph	First women Olympic Gold Medalists	Golfer, 1900 Swimmer, 1912 Diver, 1913 Figure skater, 1956 Runner, 1960
Edith Wharton	First Pulitzer Prize winner for fiction, 1921	Wrote *The Age of Innocence*
Janet Gaynor	First actress to win Academy Award, 1928	Best actress for *Seventh Heaven*
Jane Addams	First woman Nobel Peace Prize recipient, 1931	Opened Hull House for immigration and social reform
Hattie McDaniel	First African American actress to win Academy Award, 1940	Best supporting actress for *Gone with the Wind*
Gerty T. Cori	First American woman Nobel Prize winner in science, 1947	Physician and biochemist

Women Who Dared to Be Different

Marian Anderson	First African American woman to perform a major role at the Metropolitan Opera, 1955	Played Ulrica in *Un Ballo in Maschera*
Rachel Carson	First woman scientist and author to call attention to environmental issues and protection, 1962	Her book *Silent Spring* warned of the dangers of careless use of chemical pesticides and launched widespread interest in the problem of environmental pollution
Constance Baker Motley	First African American woman judge, 1966	Recommended by Senator Robert Kennedy and appointed by President Lyndon Johnson to U.S. District Court in New York
Shirley Chisholm	First African American congresswoman, 1968	U. S. House of Representatives, from New York
Emily Howell Warner	First woman pilot to fly for a commercial airline, 1973	Frontier Airlines
Robyn Smith	First woman jockey to ride in a thoroughbred stakes race, 1973	Ran in Paumonok Handicap on North Sea Horse at Aquaduct in New York
Jeanne M. Holm	First woman major general, 1973	Director of Women in the air force
Barbara Walters	First woman television news anchor, 1976	"ABC Evening News"
Janna Lambine	First woman coast guard pilot, 1977	Accepted for flight training at Naval Air Station in Pensacola, Florida
Susan B. Anthony	First woman pictured on U. S. Coin, 1979	One-dollar coin
Sandra Day O'Connor	First woman to serve on the U. S. Supreme Court	Appointed by President Ronald Reagan
Sally Ride	First American woman to fly in space, 1983	Chosen as crew member for seventh space shuttle mission
Tiffany Chin	First Chinese American figure skating winner, 1985	National Senior Ladies Figure Skating Title

Dr. Johnnetta B. Cole First African American woman president of Spelman College, 1987

Spokesperson for educational issues and human rights

Dr. Antonia Novello First Hispanic to become U.S. Surgeon General, 1989

Replaced C. Everett Koop

Dr. Jocelyn Elders First African American to become U.S. Surgeon General, 1993

Replaced Antonia Novello

 Other women I admire...

Setting Priorities, Making Choices

Setting priorities and making choices is important in any stage of life. As **Hire Learners**, your immediate choices revolve around getting an education and a job. But there is more to life than a career . . . .

A famous woman once said, "One cannot collect all the beautiful shells on the beach." In other words, you can't have everything. As new opportunities open up for women, many try to take on their new role while still meeting all the obligations of the old roles — care of the family, housework, etc. Many men are doing the reverse, trying to take on more of the woman's traditional role while still trying to be a provider.

Both men and women sometimes feel unfulfilled unless they can manage a high-paid, high-powered career; dress their children in designer fashions; be perfect, attentive spouses; entertain guests; be well-groomed; keep a spotless kitchen; and participate in school, community,

and church events. In short, they try to be superwomen and supermen.

Recently, that highly stressed mind-set has given way to a desire for balance. People today seek a healthy mix between home and work. Both female and male workers want careers that allow time to be with family and friends. They're choosing flexible work schedules, home offices, and family-run businesses — instead of higher paying corporate jobs — as a way to reduce stress and balance their lives.

Companies are becoming sensitive to this shift in the work ethic and are providing such benefits as job sharing, flex time, maternity and paternity leave, on-site day care, and parent care assistance programs. As a student of **Hire Learning**, you should consider what such programs may mean for you, and pay special attention to companies and careers that offer them.

Interviewing Women
of Influence

Here's an exercise to help you better understand the role of women in the workplace today. It takes the form of an information interview (see the guidelines discussed under "Conducting a Job Search" in Book 2 of **Hire Learning**).

The questions help you gain insight from women who are continuing their education, resuming employment after childbirth or child rearing, running their own businesses, competing in male-dominated professions, changing careers, working as single parents, breaking down racial barriers, working for wage justice, and seeking what should be the most important goals of employment: dignity, satisfaction, and fulfillment.

Arrange to interview women who are pursuing goals like those listed above. Use this form to record their answers. Investigate ways you can learn more from the women you meet. For example, perhaps you could work in an internship for one of them.

Interview Form

Person interviewed: _____

Job/career title: _____

Date: _____ Time: _____ Place: _____ Telephone: _____

Describe your present work, including how long you have been employed. _____

_____

What influenced you to enter this career field? _____

_____

What education and training is required for a person in your job/career? _____

_____

What changes do you predict will affect your job/career field in the next decade? _____

_____

What satisfies you most about your present job/career? _____

_____

Interview Form

What frustrations or stresses (if any) affect your employment? _____

_____

People say a woman has to work harder or be smarter than a man to succeed in a male-dominated profession. What's your opinion? _____

_____

Which barriers or obstacles have you personally overcome in your work or faced as a result of your work? _____

_____

What limitations or restrictions (if any) are placed on female workers in your chosen career field?

_____

What is your opinion of the increasing number of women and minorities entering the workforce?

_____

If I were to interview a male role model on the topic of "women in the workplace," what questions would you recommend I ask? _____

_____

Do you have children? What career goals do you want most for your daughter(s)? Your sons(s)?

_____

Among women you know, who has been the most important influence in your life? _____

_____

How do the media (television, video, movies, advertisements) affect your status as a female in the workplace? _____

_____

What advice do you have for young women entering your job/career field? _____

_____

Attitude Determines Altitude

Attitudes can control actions. Some women are sure they'll face resistance, resentment, and ridicule in their workplace. By beginning with a negative attitude, they limit their chances for success. They put up their own barriers.

Other women make realistic decisions about which jobs and careers they want to pursue. They investigate the education and training needed. Then they pursue those interests, without regard for the "gender agenda." They learn about laws that protect them, and they look for successful role models. They understand that they must make choices that enhance their self-esteem.

The difference in these approaches is important. Attitude does determine altitude. You can only go as high as you believe you can. That's true for both males and females studying **Hire Learning**.

To help you celebrate your positive attitude, make a collage or button that conveys your sense of worth and the positive attitudes you have. Use photos, quotations, illustrations, or poetry to record your feelings as a winner in the workplace.

 Use this space to sketch your ideas for a button or collage.

Dealing with Workplace Realities

ire Learning helps you learn about yourself, your values, and your interests, talents, and abilities. This course also teaches you about the full job search process. Your new understanding of yourself and of job searching will help you find employment and make a valuable contribution to the company that hires you.

But your training doesn't end with the words, "You're hired!" Getting a job is only the beginning. Each work site offers different experiences and demands. Each can introduce you to new values, cultures, and expectations. You may find yourself working beside people of different races, ethnic backgrounds, ages, and skill levels. Some sites will value your ability to work as a team member, encouraging a "quality circle" approach to decision making, while others reward individual initiative and creativity.

At your new job, staff meetings may be conducted in more than one language, and company publications may be bilingual too. The ethics of honesty, punctuality, and dependability will remain important, but the list of other valuable employee assets may be hard to predict — and no job description tells you how to deal with a difficult boss or an impending layoff.

Just as you need to prepare for getting a job, you also need to prepare for the diversity of people, actions, and experiences you'll find in every job you get. This section describes people in different work situations. Read each page and discuss it with your instructors, peers, and family. Put yourself in the role of each worker and ask yourself:

- Why did these problems happen?
- How could they have been avoided?
- What questions must be answered before the worker can choose a solution?

Remember that you don't need to find the "perfect" solution to problems. What counts is how you approach the problem, not exactly how you solve it.

To expand your **Hire Learning** skills, write up a page about a "people" problem you faced at work or school, write some questions about it, and have your classmates answer them. The stories in this section will serve as examples.

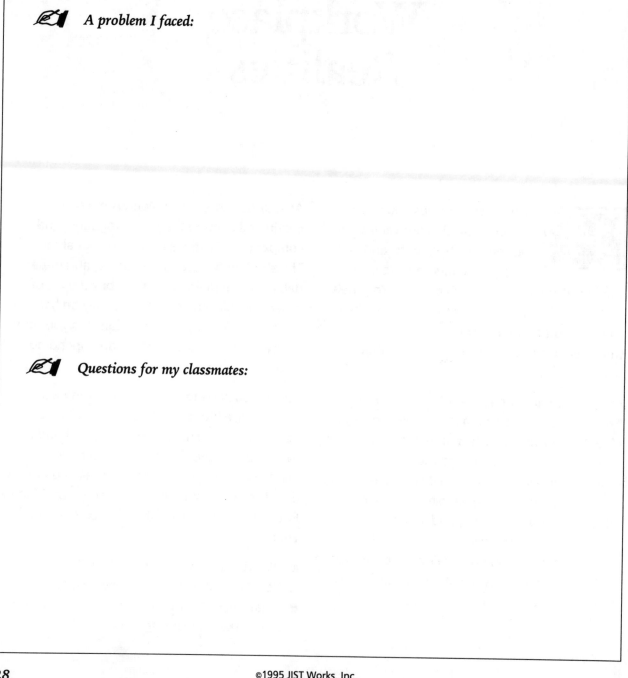

✍ *A problem I faced:*

✍ *Questions for my classmates:*

Just a Thank You, Please!

Joyce is a research assistant for a small marine science laboratory that specializes in investigating water pollution. She wants to pursue this as her life's career, so she's working hard to earn enough money to continue her education in environmental science.

Joyce's supervisor, Dr. Hobbs, was also her interviewer and got Joyce hired. Joyce has always felt that they have a productive, professional relationship. In the past, Dr. Hobbs often encouraged Joyce about her career plans and seemed genuinely interested in helping Joyce expand her skills.

However, in the last three months, Dr. Hobbs has changed. She's not that friendly anymore, to Joyce or anyone else. Everything is all business! Sometimes she's abrupt and too critical. She moves around the lab speaking to no one, and she rarely smiles.

Joyce is uncomfortable now. She worries that Dr. Hobbs is hiding some problem with the lab, like a cut in funds. Since she's one of the youngest employees, Joyce knows she would probably be the first to be laid off. She wonders if her work is satisfactory. She never gets a please or thank you from Dr. Hobbs when she has stayed extra hours to get a project in by a tight deadline.

Last weekend, Joyce told her boyfriend, "I can't stand the lack of communication. More work every day, and no way of knowing what's wrong. I don't know how much longer I can stand this cold, impersonal place! And I'm not the only one who's feeling the cold chill!"

- Obviously Joyce is hurt, disappointed, and confused. Do you think she's looking for worker recognition, or is there a deeper need? Explain your answer.
- Do you think Joyce should confront Dr. Hobbs and explain her feelings? What would she say? Predict Dr. Hobbs's reaction.
- How could holding employee conferences from time to time help solve this communication problem?
- Take Dr. Hobbs's side, and list possible reasons for her behavior.
- What do you think will happen to the lab's productivity if the present problem continues?
- Research some of the current practices for making employees feel appreciated and recognized.

 Use this space to record your thoughts.

The Pink Slip . . . Why Me?

 Patricia was so excited! She had just finished a meeting with the job placement director at Green Oaks High School. Mr. Goldberg told Pat about a part-time job opening at a local farm stand. In that job, she would harvest and clean the fruits and vegetables, display them attractively, and wait on customers. Pat could hardly wait for school to end so she could get into her work clothes to go out and make some money.

Through late June and early July, the job was super! But then heavy rains damaged some crops. Business at the stand slumped. When Pat got her paycheck for the first week in August, a "pink slip" was also in the envelope, saying she was fired. She couldn't believe her eyes! "Why me? I've been working hard! Why should I be fired? It just doesn't make sense!"

Pat went straight to Sue Kelly, the owner. She burst into tears and asked why she should be fired. She told Ms. Kelly she had not missed a single day of work, and often worked overtime when fragile fruits had to be cleaned and refrigerated.

Ms. Kelly just shrugged her shoulders and replied, "Business is in a slump now. I have more help than I can afford. You HAVE been a fine worker. I never had to keep an eye on you. But you were the last one hired, so you have to be the first to be laid off." Pat couldn't hold back her frustration. "So that's the treatment I get when I try to do my best?"

- How can a new employee adjust to the "last one hired — first one fired" rule?
- What questions could Pat have asked in her job interview that would have better prepared her for what happened?
- How do people who have financial and family responsibilities cope when they get laid off?
- Should Pat ask Ms. Kelly to write a letter of recommendation to help her get another job? How could Ms. Kelly have been more sensitive to Pat's feelings and her obvious disappointment?

 Use this space to record your thoughts.

All in the Family

The Giardano family has owned the sandwich shop ever since the new mall opened 10 years ago. Mr. Giardano has always been proud of running a family business. His grandfather and father before him owned family restaurants in Italy. But as his business has grown, Mr. Giardano has had to hire other employees, some not in the family.

Vincent, Mr. Giardano's youngest son, has started work at the shop, clearing tables. At first it was fun, and being the boss's son made the job easier, or so Vincent thought. "Other employees don't hassle you. They know better!" Vincent told his buddy, Al.

But lately, Vincent feels clearing tables is a bore. He wishes for a job with more responsibility. He resents having to clean up other people's messes. And now, he sometimes talks on the phone to Al when he should be clearing tables. Last week, Vincent took off on Friday's lunch shift, the busiest shift of the week. He didn't warn anyone — he just didn't show up. Instead he took off to the amusement park.

His coworkers were swamped with extra work, and they were angry. After work, they met in the parking lot and decided to complain to Mr. Giardano. "Why should we cover for Vincent?" they said. "I don't care if he IS the boss's son. We've got our rights, too!" However, one worker warned, "You know Mr. Giardano thinks his kids can do no wrong. Will he fire us for complaining about his own kid?"

- If you owned a business, how would you deal with worker complaints or conflicts?
- If you were Mr. Giardano, how would you have prepared Vincent for his job?
- Do you think that Vincent took advantage because he was the boss's son? Explain your answer.
- If you were the boss's son or daughter, would you want to work for your parents? What extra responsibilities come with being a member of the family business?
- How do you think Mr. Giardano will handle the complaints of his employees?

 Use this space to record your thoughts.

I Just Don't Fit In!

va Ruiz was proud when she landed her first job as a receptionist in a computer firm. Her friendliness — a definite "people skill" — impressed the personnel manager who hired her. Eva is the first person in her family to get a job since the family moved to America from Mexico two months ago. She learned English before the move, so she speaks both English and Spanish. She still needs to become familiar with the figures of speech used in America, and she needs to learn more about the computer terminology used at her new company.

But Eva wonders if she sought a job too quickly. She feels that she really doesn't have much in common with her coworkers. Some of them miss the previous receptionist, an older woman who mothered everyone. Eva has tried hard to be friendly with others, and she's also been trying to prove herself to her boss. But now coworkers have said things to her, such as "Don't work so hard! You want to make the rest of us look bad? You must be pushing for a raise!"

Eva doesn't understand the attitudes of her coworkers. In Mexico, she remembers hearing of America as a land of opportunity where hard work led to success. She has thought about quitting, but she promised that she would try to earn enough money to help her married sister's family come to the United States too.

- Who has the attitude problem in this situation?
- What is the real reason the coworkers are bothered by Eva?
- What could Eva do to improve her relationship with her coworkers?
- What is the best way to handle office gossip and distrust among workers?

 Use this space to record your thoughts.

The Price of Popularity

Alice was recently hired as a hostess in a small restaurant. Her professional appearance, good grooming, and outgoing personality got her the job.

Alice wants to do a good job. She arrives at work one-half hour early. Often, she helps the waiters and waitresses clear the tables when there's a rush. Diners have told the manager that they like Alice's personality. Some customers even ask for her when she is not on duty.

But now, a rumor is going around. Someone's saying that Alice has tried to take away part of the waiter's or waitress's tip when she has helped them. Another story is that Alice becomes overly friendly to try to get bigger tips. Suddenly, her friendliness to customers is seen as competition for tips. Since her wages are low compared to other jobs, the tips are an important part of her income. But because of the rumors, a group of waitresses and a bartender are planning to confront the manager about her.

- If you were the manager, how might you handle the tip issue?
- If you were the manager and you heard a complaint about Alice or any of your employees, how would you handle the situation?
- Do you feel that the manager is at fault for not making strict rules about Alice's job and who gets the tips?
- Do you think that Alice is greedy and sneaky or just hard-working? Explain your answer.
- If you were Alice's friend and also her coworker, how could you help her with the other workers?

 Use this space to record your thoughts.

Dress for Success

Jubae was always one of the best-dressed girls in her class. She always wore the latest fashions and accessories. Her teachers thought some of her clothes were rather extreme, but she certainly got attention. Jubae always saved up her money to buy different outfits for every season.

Jubae has just been hired as a hospitality coordinator for a fancy hotel chain. Her ability to speak several languages is one reason she got the job. Jubae is friendly and finds it easy to meet and greet new people. Unfortunately, her clothes are too wild for the hotel. The hotel guests dress in business clothes, and the other hotel employees meet a strict dress code. Jubae is not allowed to wear her flashy clothes at work. She doesn't enjoy dressing conservatively, and that's making her irritable on the job — a job in which she's supposed to be friendly.

- Can employers force workers to meet a dress code?
- How does clothing affect work tasks and responsibilities?
- Discuss how what you wear — colors, styles, etc. — affects your self-esteem.
- How should Jubae respond when her supervisor tells her that her clothes are wrong for her job?
- Would you tell Jubae to propose changes in the dress code? Why? Why not?

 Use this space to record your thoughts.

Responsible Parent or Responsible Worker?

laire has always been good at selling. When she was a little girl, she sold lemonade at her own stand. She won first prize — a trip to Disney World — for selling the most newspaper subscriptions in her town. Now, at age 37, Claire has made it to the "big time" in selling — she sells to millions of people on a TV home shopping network.

Claire takes her work seriously. She takes pride in her appearance, she's always on time, she meets her deadlines, and she hardly ever takes a day off, even when she's sick. But since her divorce, the pressures of caring for her five children — ages five to 14 — are wearing her down.

The children are at an age when school activities are important — plays, pageants, field trips, concerts. Claire wants to attend these special activities but finds it hard to get the time off from work. This spring, Claire's eight-year-old had the lead in a play. Claire asked for time off to go to the play, and her supervisor said okay. Then Stephen won an athletic trophy. Claire requested time off again. The supervisor said okay but added, "I hope this doesn't become a habit. I've got a show to run and you're needed on the set." Now it's time for a parent-teacher conference that can only be scheduled during work hours. What's worse, the kids have been calling the network because they're lonely when they get home from school.

Claire is a good mother and a good worker, but she knows that the conflict between her work time and her parenting is a growing problem. Other employees are also beginning to resent the times Claire takes off. When she goes, they have to work harder to make up Claire's work. And sometimes, Claire's gone longer than she said she would be. The parent conference was supposed to last a half-hour, but it ended up taking two hours. Claire offered to work extra hours to make up the time, but that didn't satisfy her annoyed coworkers.

- What are a person's responsibilities to family and to work? Can they be separated?
- If you were Claire's supervisor, what would you do the next time Claire asks for time off because of family responsibilities?
- What can Claire do to smooth over the problems with her boss and her coworkers?

 Use this space to record your thoughts.

Out of Control

ech started work two months ago as a construction worker on a bridge repair project. Being a strong man, Lech was happy to have a job where he could work outdoors and use his muscles productively. He's making good money at his job.

Lech's problem, though, is that he is hot-tempered. All his life, people have tried to help him control his temper, but somehow he has always slipped back into the habit of defending his "rights" with his fists.

Last week, he accidentally moved a crane in the wrong direction. He yanked at the controls angrily and knocked over some pilings that had been set up just the day before. A coworker yelled in frustration, and Lech's boss shouted, "When are you ever going to learn how to do this job and stop making such dumb mistakes?"

Seething, Lech grabbed his boss by the throat and cursed him out. Not surprisingly, Lech was fired on the spot.

- Do you believe that Lech's firing was fair?
- How do you think Lech felt after he was fired?
- What could Lech do to learn how to control his temper?
- How will Lech explain the reason he left this job when he interviews for his next job?

 Use this space to record your thoughts.

Honesty Is the Best Policy

Audrey has always enjoyed working with machines and engines. Now just 17 years old, she's landed her first part-time job in a gas station. Audrey's goal is one day to manage her own gas station and to train young people who enjoy this type of work. She would also like to restore antique cars.

Things were going well for Audrey in her first job. But the manager, who had hired Audrey on the recommendation of her neighbor, decided to test her honesty. He slipped an extra $20 into the cash register on a day when Audrey would be responsible for adding up the receipts and making sure that the total matched the amount in the register. Her records should have shown that there was $20 too much in the register. But the next day, Audrey reported that everything added up perfectly — meaning she took the $20.

The manager has decided to fire Audrey, even though she apologized and explained that she was short on cash and wanted to go on a weekend trip with friends.

- Why do you think the manager felt he needed to test Audrey's honesty?
- Make a list of thoughts Audrey may have had before she "borrowed" the $20.
- Is there another way that the manager could have tested Audrey's honesty?
- Do you think that Audrey should have been fired, even though this was her first offense? Explain your answer.
- Explain how Audrey should answer questions in her next job interview about her honesty or why she left her previous job.
- How do you feel about honesty tests that employers give workers?

 Use this space to record your thoughts.

Ricardo Versus Control

 Ricardo is enrolled in a school that has an internship program. Ricardo really enjoys working with young children. Because of this interest, he got an internship at a day care center.

At the center, the children flock to Ricardo because of his fun personality. However, his supervisor has noticed that the children have trouble settling down after playing under Ricardo's supervision. The day care center director has spoken to Ricardo and suggested ways that Ricardo can help children move smoothly from one activity to another. But still, the children are unmanageable after working with Ricardo.

Other workers resent the way the children enjoy Ricardo, and now Ricardo is beginning to feel uncomfortable. What started out as a positive experience is becoming a frustration. Ricardo had been looking at catalogs of colleges where he might major in early childhood education, but now he's having second thoughts.

- What's the real problem in this situation?
- Is the problem with the children really Ricardo's fault?
- How would you tell Ricardo to fix the problem with his supervisor? With his coworkers?
- Where could Ricardo go to learn how to help the children learn better self-control?
- Describe an event in your life that started out positive and turned bad. How did you handle the problem?
- How can the problem be solved without ruining Ricardo's interest in working with young children?

 Use this space to record your thoughts.

Following the Boss's Orders

Mi Ling has always been interested in how things work, so she chose the electrical course at school. Her instructor, Mrs. Kline, has complimented her on her aptitude, her ability to follow directions, and her desire to learn the skills needed by an electronics technician. Mrs. Kline suggested that Mi Ling get a part-time summer job working with electrical and electronic machines.

Mi Ling's first interview was with a repair shop. Thanks to Mrs. Kline's recommendation, she was hired. Mi Ling was told that her work would vary, depending on what was needed most. Sometimes she would wait on customers. Other times she would make repairs on televisions, video equipment, computers, and appliances. The variety appealed to Mi Ling.

But Mi Ling's boss noticed quickly that she was very good with customers. He began to give Mi Ling more days at the front desk and fewer working on repairs. By fall, Mi Ling had made only a few minor repairs. She knew that the school year would soon be starting, and she asked herself, "What have I learned in this job? I've enjoyed working with people, but what skills have I learned for my goals? Someday, I want to be a robotics service technician and perhaps design machines for underwater exploration."

- Mi Ling certainly had an admirable work goal. How could she have told her boss about her desire to learn new technical skills?
- Do you think Mi Ling's problem is her own fault because she didn't mention her frustration to her boss earlier in the summer? Why or why not?
- What skills has Mi Ling developed in this summer job?
- How could these skills be used to her advantage in future jobs?
- List some ways that Mi Ling can learn new skills during the school year.
- Scan the classified ads to find some places that you think Mi Ling should apply to next summer.

 Use this space to record your thoughts.

Juggling School and Work Time

 im Fong, age 15, earns $40 to $60 in tips at a neighborhood restaurant every weekend. She loves the money, because it helps her buy clothes and also helps support her mother and three younger sisters. But Kim also works every evening after school. She works hard at her jobs, and now her grades at the local technical school are suffering because she's tired and doesn't have time to do her homework.

Trevor King was hired last summer as a dishwasher at a hotel. Trevor wasn't excited about washing dishes all summer, but it was a way to earn money for college and to keep his run-down car on the road. Soon Trevor was promoted to short-order cook and was working right up until time to return to school. Trevor was earning more than he had hoped for, so he decided to keep his job during school, while still trying to stay on the school's honor roll. He's not doing very well. Trevor failed two classes in the first semester! He's shocked, and his parents are frustrated and disappointed.

Both Kim and Trevor have a strong work ethic, but their school work is suffering because the lure of money and independence are taking time away from their education. They also don't get enough sleep to concentrate properly, and haven't the time to enjoy important after-school activities.

- How do you feel about working part-time during school?
- Should there be a limit on the number of hours a student should be allowed to work? Please explain.
- What health hazards or other risks could you face when working with equipment or with little supervision?
- Research child labor laws to learn about young people working illegally or injuries they got from their jobs. What types of work settings tend to violate child labor laws the most?
- Pretend you are a parent and have a son or daughter who wants to work while in junior high or high school. What rules would you make about your own children's jobs?

 Use this space to record your thoughts.

Romantic Rivalry

fter working for three months as a secretary in her first job, Betty was flattered to find she was getting extra attention from the department's director. Mr. Case, who was 15 years older than Betty, often chatted with her about matters unrelated to her work. Once, he invited her to a coffee shop after work.

Betty believed that she was doing well in her first job, and she was pleased that her efforts were noticed. She was confused, therefore, when her immediate supervisor began finding fault with Betty's work. The supervisor, Ms. Joyce, was rumored to be secretly dating Mr. Case.

Upset, Betty asked her coworkers about the quality of her work and was reassured that she was doing well. But after she got more harsh criticism from Ms. Joyce, Betty decided she had no choice but to quit.

- Why do you think Ms. Joyce is so critical of Betty?
- Should Betty go around Ms. Joyce and complain to Mr. Case? Why? Why not?
- If Betty confronts Ms. Joyce, how should she explain her feelings of frustration?
- If you were Betty, would you quit? Why? Why not?
- What questions should an employee ask him or herself before choosing to quit a job?

 Use this space to record your thoughts.

Treading on Tradition

Juan was excited about his summer job. He was looking forward to working at the local paper mill before heading off to college. He felt that he needed some hands-on experience to go along with the business management program he planned to major in.

After a week on the job, Juan went to his supervisor with an idea that could speed up the mill. Juan's figures showed that by adding one more person to the staff, production could be increased by 25 percent and the mill's profits would go up.

The supervisor took Juan over to the lead assembler, who immediately shot down Juan's idea. The supervisor told Juan, "These folks know more about production than you'll ever learn at college. Trying to be a one-week wonder won't win you any friends around here." The assembler added, "You do your job, and we'll do ours. After all, we've been doing this for years. We don't need your bright ideas."

Juan still felt his plan would work, but he knew he couldn't win. He could also tell that it was going to be a long summer.

- Do you think Juan should look for another job?
- What can Juan do to show his coworkers that he's not trying to "show them up"?
- How can Juan find other work opportunities where his desire for self-improvement and increased productivity will be appreciated?
- Think about a situation where you had a way to solve a problem or an opportunity to make a difference. Did you feel you could speak your mind, or did you feel pressure to be one of the crowd and abandon your own creativity? What did you do?

 Use this space to record your thoughts.

No Disrespect

Alfonso Rambis loved cars. He now had his first job, working at a large auto center. He was the "new guy," so he was responsible for everything from pumping gas and changing oil to unpacking new auto supplies and getting coffee. "Just call me Coach, kid," said the station manager on Alfonso's first day. "Nice to have you on board, Al." "Pleased to meet you, Sir," said Alfonso. "My name is Alfonso. I'm excited about this job." "Okay, Alfonso, make sure you sweep out those service bays before the mechanics begin their work," said the Coach.

Later that morning, Alfonso met Miguel, Bolts, Johnny, and Lefty. Although he told them his name was Alfonso Rambis, he got called all sorts of things: Al, the Kid, Alfie, and even Rambo! After two days on the job, he began to cringe when his name was called. He felt the others were making fun of him. When his uniform arrived on Friday, "Al" was the name sewn on the blue shirt.

One coworker told him the Coach used to play minor league baseball and thought of his workers as a team. "His nicknames are a sign of affection. You'll get used to it."

- Why do you think Alfonso wants to be called by his full name?
- Could the use of nicknames be related to a casual attitude about employer-employee relationships? Explain your answer.
- How would you tell Alfonso to discuss the situation with Coach?
- How could Alfonso's feelings affect his relationships with Miguel, Bolts, Johnny, and Lefty?
- Identify other types of jobs where Alfonso might not have this problem.
- Explain how a person's full name is "advertised" as part of the work environment.

 Use this space to record your thoughts.

Worker Overload

Gerry just started working as a paralegal. The paralegal profession is giving Gerry a chance to learn more about law, which has always fascinated her. The five lawyers in the firm make heavy demands on her time. Even though Gerry has another paralegal working with her, the work load is becoming too much.

Also, the office environment has become tense and pressure-packed. One attorney always seems to be in a bad mood and takes out his anger on the paralegals and secretaries. Another young attorney has been a little too friendly with Gerry, making her feel uncomfortable. The heavy work load, plus the stress Gerry is experiencing with office relationships, is really overwhelming her.

Gerry views this job as a test for whether she might like to pursue a law degree. In high school, she was warned about the pressures of jobs like this. But she thought the warnings were all just theories. Now she knows what pressure means, and she's having second thoughts about practicing law.

- How does a worker refuse extra work responsibilities in a polite but assertive manner?
- What risks are involved in asserting your rights as an employee?
- Will leaving this law firm and seeking a job at a different law firm solve the problem for Gerry?
- Is there any way that Gerry could have anticipated these problems before she accepted the position?
- What advice do you have for Gerry and her coworker?

 Use this space to record your thoughts.

Do You Really Know Me?

Sara is 18 and a senior. A couple of years ago, she almost quit school. It seemed then that her whole life was falling apart. Her parents had just divorced. She had broken up with her boyfriend, and her grades were terrible! She also got involved with a crowd that was into drugs.

But a close call in a serious automobile accident turned things around for Sara. With the help of her parents and her guidance counselor, she began to get back on track. Sara knew that without a high school diploma, she'd have trouble finding a decent job.

Sara is working part-time in a department store as a sales clerk. She got a bonus during the winter holiday season and takes her job responsibilities seriously. The store has offered her a job about 100 miles from her home after she graduates.

Sara is excited about the opportunity to learn from the job she was offered. A couple of years ago, she wouldn't have dreamt she could get a chance like this. She likes the idea of being independent and on her own. But she's also scared to be on her own. She knows she'll probably have to share her apartment with others to pay the rent. How will her roommates influence her, once she's away from the family? Will her old high school troubles return and foul up this great opportunity?

- Sara has several problems. Which one should she address first?
- If you were Sara, would you discuss your fears about a new lifestyle with the supervisor of the new job? Why? Why not?
- What can Sara do to feel better about being on her own?
- Where can Sara get some lifestyle management skills?
- What can she do to find a suitable roommate?

 Use this space to record your thoughts.

Office Pettiness
and Politics

 G ina has been with Best Footwear Corporation for four months as a data communications specialist. She really enjoys her work. Best Corporation is close to her parent's home, so she's saving money by commuting. The cash she saves by not renting her own place will help her improve her skills at a nearby community college.

But an unexpected situation has arisen at work. Several of Gina's coworkers seem to be avoiding her. They sit together at break. They are polite to Gina, but also cool. Gina has tried to be friendly with them, with no real success. Although she feels left out and uncomfortable, they haven't done anything so bad that she can complain to her supervisor. After all, they haven't actually violated company rules or regulations.

Just last week, sitting alone at lunch, Gina glanced up and saw a group of her coworkers entering the computer room. At first, she panicked. "Was I supposed to be at a lunch meeting?" thought Gina. Quickly checking her calendar, she saw that there was no meeting. Then suddenly, Gina was brought out of her thoughts by the singing of "Happy Birthday, Mr. Stout . . . ." Mr. Stout is her division supervisor, but no one had told her about the party.

Becoming an insider is more difficult than it appears. Gina was taught to work hard and show a positive attitude. Now office politics are getting in her way.

- What are some possible reasons why Gina is being left out by her coworkers?
- If you were Gina, how would you handle this situation? Go into the computer room as if you were invited? Cry and not return to work the next day? Pretend to be sick and ask to go home early? Start looking for another job?
- If this problem continues, would you recommend that Gina complain to her supervisor? Why? Why not?
- List some ways Gina can survive in a difficult work environment that also matches her skills and financial goals.

 Use this space to record your thoughts.

Handling Disappointment

 ola, a junior in high school, has joined a school-to-work transition program this semester. After a self-assessment process in which they discuss their interests, abilities, and aptitudes, students intern at work sites where their interests and abilities can be enhanced.

Lola has always been interested in interior design, so when she learned that there was an opening with a furniture company, she couldn't wait for her visitation days. She was instructed to report to Lois Short at the company. That was extra exciting, because Ms. Short writes a decorating column for the local newspaper.

On the first day of the internship, Lola dressed tastefully and arrived at the furniture company 10 minutes early. Lola met the receptionist and announced herself. The receptionist said, "Oh, yes, I think I heard you were coming today. Ms. Short isn't back from lunch yet. Why don't you sit over there and read a magazine until she arrives."

Lola felt uncomfortable, disappointed, and frustrated. "What a way to start the internship!"

Shifting from one foot to another, she made her way to the lounge area and slumped down in the chair. Fifteen minutes passed, a half-hour passed. After 40 minutes, Lola left.

The next day at school, Lola's mentor called Lola into her office. She asked why Ms. Short's office reported that Lola had not completed her first intern day. Lola told her side of the story and said, "If they don't care enough to plan for me, I don't care to learn about their business! Let's forget the whole thing. Every time I plan for something special I'm always disappointed anyway!"

- How would you describe Lola's response to the missed appointment?
- Do you think she was right to leave? Why? Why not?
- What could the mentor do to prevent this from happening to another intern?
- Could Ms. Short's receptionist have eased Lola's discomfort? How?
- If Lola's internship was a real job interview instead, and she arrived for the interview only to find that the interviewer was unavailable, how should she handle the situation?

 Use this space to record your thoughts.

Be There — On Time!

Carl remembers the lectures he got when he was in high school about not doing assignments on time. His teachers were always saying, "Good work habits become automatic, and poor work habits persist unless a person makes an effort to turn things around." But Carl admits that their warnings never really sunk in. He still puts things off, showing up late and handing in work well past the deadline.

Now Carl has worked for the Ace Telephone Answering Service for six months. In his job, he must stick to a strict time schedule since Ace provides 24-hour service.

Recently, all the lectures he heard in high school have come back to haunt him. Mr. Holley called Carl into his office last week and shouted, "Late again! What's your excuse this time?" Before Carl could answer, Mr. Holley continued, "Your time sheet shows that you've been late nine times during the past month! I've also had two complaints from other workers that you are extending your work break a few minutes longer each time you work the night shift. Don't you know that time is money? Didn't anyone ever teach you about punctuality? When you're late, it affects everyone else's work schedule! I'm giving you one more chance. If you're late again, you're fired."

- Given Carl's history, do you think the boss's threat will work? Why? Why not?
- What type of training or counseling in high school programs helps students who lack self-discipline?
- Carl was trained for this job at the interview, and a coworker spent about a half-hour with Carl on his first day — that was all. How could Ace help new workers understand the importance of time commitments through better training?
- How could Mr. Holley have handled Carl's lateness more humanely?

 Use this space to record your thoughts.

The College Dropout

eter always excelled in math and science while he was in school, and he thought he wanted to be a pharmacist. His dad really supported and encouraged Peter's career choice. Right after high school, Peter was accepted at a college of pharmacy.

Peter made it through only two years at the college. During that time, his dad died, and the loss affected Peter greatly. He felt he didn't have any reason to try any more. Besides, organic chemistry was really difficult, and lately the prestige of "pushing pills" had worn thin for Peter. He finally told his mom that he was quitting school. His mom, sad and lonely, didn't put up a fuss. She thought it was just one more stroke of bad luck.

Peter carelessly looked through the newspaper. He had taken computer courses in school, so when he found a position as a computer systems analyst, he said, "Why not go for it?" The interview went well, and Peter was hired — but for less pay than he expected.

Although he's overqualified and underpaid, Peter enjoys what he is doing. Already he's updated some of the company's computer programs — which saved the company a lot of money. Without Peter, the company would have had to hire an expensive consultant. A casual comment was made once about paying Peter to complete his college degree while working there, but after nine months, nothing more has been said about it.

- What are the risks in choosing someone else's career plans for yourself?
- How could Peter and his family have learned about other options for his future?
- How do you think employers react when they interview a college dropout?
- How long do you think Peter will enjoy his work in a situation where he's underpaid?
- How can Peter avoid the mistake of entering college without a definite career goal once again?

 Use this space to record your thoughts.

A Difficult Boss

yle has always been interested in health-related occupations. Even as a young child, Kyle wanted to take care of his younger brothers and sisters when they were sick. It had been Kyle's secret ambition to be a doctor, but his grades weren't good enough. Kyle worked hard in school, but he still struggled.

Kyle took his first full-time job — as a custodian at a small hospital — after graduation from high school. Kyle enjoyed it at first. He worked hard and had an understanding supervisor — until last month. The man who had hired Kyle resigned, and the new supervisor always seems to find fault with Kyle. The other day he barked, "Can't you do a better job mopping these floors? Looks like you cleaned those corners with your eyes closed!" Last week, the supervisor saw Kyle casually talking to one of the lab technicians. He approached Kyle angrily and snapped, "Am I paying you to make friends? The Pediatrics Examining Room needs a lightbulb replaced! Get moving!" Kyle was embarrassed and angry. Last Friday he almost told the supervisor off — but he needs the job. Besides, he was doing so well before the old supervisor left.

- Kyle feels unappreciated, but he needs a job and his work puts him in an environment where he feels he can make a difference. How is he going to deal with the verbal abuse and put-downs if he stays in this job?
- If he quits, how will Kyle explain it when he goes for another job interview?
- Would Kyle be better off if he asked for a change in shift to a time when a different supervisor was on duty? In what way could this be an advantage?
- Should Kyle discuss his problem with the manager who oversees all the supervisors? What if the personnel manager agrees with the supervisor? What then?

 Use this space to record your thoughts.

Having It All!

Samantha grew up in a family of medical careers. Her older brother just received a degree in clinical psychology. Her dad and two uncles all practice medicine. Now Samantha wants to become a doctor.

She knows she's facing some obstacles, because she's entering a profession still dominated by men. As a child reading about the lives of important doctors who were women, she learned that "attitude determines altitude." She planned to study, work hard, and be happy in her work.

But Samantha wasn't totally prepared for the problems she has encountered. Samantha is divorced and has twin daughters, age five. Her family background is traditional — mothers staying home and caring for their children. Right after her divorce, Samantha relied on her mother to babysit when the round-the-clock demands of medical school took up all her time. But it was too much for her mom, so now the twins go to preschool and then to a babysitter. Her family is complaining about the children being raised by "strangers." Samantha is stressed and feeling guilty. Now she's beginning to have doubts about the career path she has dreamed of for years. "It just wasn't supposed to be this way," Samantha told her chief of staff.

- How would you describe Samantha's problem?
- What child care choices are available for single parents?
- How can Samantha get along better with her family?
- Find out about organizations that could help Samantha with child care.
- Should Samantha give up her medical career? Why? Why not?

 Use this space to record your thoughts.

Treat Me Fairly

 Maria is employed as a typesetter in a book publishing company. She got the job through the recommendation of her business education teacher. He was impressed with her accuracy in word processing and her ability to format text in pleasing designs.

Because of her attention to detail and her ability to spot content errors, the editors soon trusted Maria to do a careful job with their typesetting. But her manager, Ms. Gross, was not a good supervisor. When typesetting needed to be done, Ms. Gross allowed the editors to bring their copy to any typesetter, without making sure that each typesetter got the same amount of work to do.

Friendly, outgoing, and accurate, Maria began to get more typesetting than her coworkers. The work began to pile up and as it did, her coworkers were getting jealous of her popularity. But they also had more free time.

Finally Maria couldn't take the stress anymore. She wanted to do a good job. She wanted to keep up with the workload, but it was too much.

The last straw came when she found out that one of her coworkers was making more money than Maria, but doing less work!

- Maria enjoys her work but doesn't like people to take advantage of her good nature or her work skills. How can she tell Ms. Gross about her frustration?
- Just as the coworkers are getting jealous of Maria, Maria is now getting jealous because one of them makes more money than she does. How can jealousy destroy the drive to do good work?
- How can a worker deal with jealousy in a constructive way?
- What if the publishing company involved all the staff in planning how work is to get done. How would that help prevent problems like Maria's?
- Since Maria is now unhappy with her job, could a promotion be a way to meet her needs and also keep her skills at the company? Plan a way for Maria to ask for a promotion and raise in pay.

 Use this space to record your thoughts.

Prejudice Rears Its Ugly Head

 anuel, age 21, was recently hired as a driver for an express mail carrier. He's thrilled to have a steady job because he has a newborn baby daughter, so he needs a steady income. Dropping out of high school is probably the worst thing that Manuel could have done, but at the time, he just couldn't take school any more. Luckily, he's done okay since then, and today he is as proud of his new family as he is of his African American heritage. He works hard at his job — his route covers 15 towns — and since he was hired three months ago, Manuel hasn't missed a day of work.

But last week was a disaster! His pick-up records didn't match with his deliveries. A large shipment of glass was damaged, and he had a fight with a coworker over a conversation he heard where a derogatory word was used about him. To make matters worse, his boss chewed him out about the pick-ups and the damaged goods. His boss shouted, "I should have known better than to hire a black! The guys told me you'd be nothing but trouble!"

- If you were Manuel, how would you respond to the boss's insult?
- Could Manuel have known before he took the job that the boss or some of his coworkers might be racists?
- What can Manuel do to improve his relationships with other drivers?
- Do you think Manuel should look for another job? Why? Why not?

 Use this space to record your thoughts.

Circumstantial Evidence

 harlie wanted to become a police officer. He grew up in a tough neighborhood, and took care of his younger brothers and sisters while his mother supported them all.

Charlie studied hard and avoided the gangs and other problems that surrounded him. He made it into the police academy and graduated at the top of his class. His first big assignment was to go back to his old neighborhood and go undercover with his partner, Paul, to try to fight the growing drug trade there.

Paul was older than Charlie and had been on the force for 10 years. He also had grown up in the neighborhood. So Charlie and Paul had a lot in common . . . or so it seemed. But one night, everything seemed to fall apart.

Charlie didn't want to believe what he had suspected for some time — but it seemed to be true. Paul might be hooked on drugs! Paul had been really edgy and stressed out lately.

Last night, as they were coming off a long stakeout, Charlie and Paul opened their lockers to change clothes and leave their weapons. When Paul opened his locker, a paper bag fell on the floor, and vials of something that looked like crack cocaine spilled out in front of Charlie. Paul quickly scooped up the stuff and remarked, "Got this stuff to give a drug prevention seminar to students at P. S. 181 next week! These kids sure need to clean up their act and leave this stuff alone. It's lethal!"

- Does Charlie have enough proof to confront Paul?
- What could happen to Charlie if he's wrong about Paul?
- How can drug use affect the partners' relationship and effectiveness?
- If you were in Charlie's place, whom would you tell? The supervisor? The police physician? Other officers? No one?

 Use this space to record your thoughts.

Are You Really Who You Appear To Be?

 veryone has a role to play in life's drama. For example, in school, some people play "the student," always trying to please the teacher. Some students play "the clown," always looking for a laugh and taking a casual attitude toward learning. You also know Mr. or Ms. "know-it-all," who puts everybody off by playing the superior role. Every school has role-players: the athlete, the party animal, the punk, the grind, and the one who plays the "I don't care about anything or anyone" role.

A role is meant to make a certain impression. That is why our roles change when we interact with different groups of people. For example, students often play a different role with their parents than they do with their peers. A person can play "the student" in class, but with friends can play "the daredevil" or "the clown." People in charge may play "the boss," but when facing a task they don't know how to do, the same people may play "helpless" to avoid embarrassment.

Sometimes, we box ourselves into corners by playing roles that don't really fit with who we are. We mask our true feelings, and choose a role that we think will impress somebody, when what matters is who we really are. Our role may blur the line between reality and fantasy and trap us into limited ways of thinking and behaving.

Think about the roles you play: at home, in school, and with friends. Choose three of your roles and decide how they may help you — or hinder you — now or in the future. List the roles, and then describe a situation in which this role is either a positive or negative role for you.

✍ *Positive Roles I Play*   *Situations*

✍ *Negative Roles I Play*   *Situations*

Now imagine you're in your first job. You've done all the right things: You looked for a position that matched your skills and interests. You filled out the application form carefully and attached a resume to it. You did well in the job interview, playing the "serious and mature" role. Now you're on the job, and other people are playing roles. Some of the roles are positive and make you feel comfortable. Other roles make you feel uneasy and unsure of yourself.

Describe how you would act in the following situations.

Situation	*Your Reaction/Role*
Supervisor plays an OVERBEARING role by saying, "You won't last long in this job! I've seen irresponsible people like you before!"	
Coworker plays a WORD TO THE WISE role by saying, "Kiss up to the boss. That's the only way you'll survive around here."	
Supervisor plays the JEALOUS role by saying, "So you're the 90-day wonder the manager has been bragging about. Well, just watch your step and remember, I'm in charge."	
On-the-job training manager plays the HELPFUL role. "Just come to me if you have any problems. That's why I'm here — to help you learn."	
Coworker plays the REBEL role by saying, "What this place needs is a complete overhaul! Let's organize a strike. We can make signs that say Minority Rule!"	
Coworker plays the TESTING role by asking, "Want to get wasted after work? Everybody does it!"	
Supervisor plays the GOSSIP role by saying, "You'll never believe what I heard about your boss . . . ."	

Situation	Your Reaction/Role
Manager plays the STRESSED role by asking, "Can't you move faster? This shipment must be on the loading docks in an hour!"	
Employer plays the COMPLIMENTARY role by saying, "I've been watching your work. You're doing a fine job. Keep it up and we'll have to think about a promotion for you."	
Best friend plays a CASUAL role by saying, "Why are you working so hard? They won't appreciate you any more! Anybody can be replaced!"	
Coworker plays the OVERWORKED role by saying, "I'm so stressed and I've got another day's work when I get home! Could you help me get my work done?"	
Friend plays the ADVICE GIVER role by saying, "The way you get appreciated around here is to throw your weight around! Let them know you aren't going to be stepped on!"	
Personnel director plays the INQUISITIVE role by saying, "You haven't seen Wanda this morning, have you? Seems like she's never around when I need her."	
Coworker plays the CONFIDANTE role by saying, "You're having problems with your boss? Tell me all about your performance review. You know I'll never tell anyone."	
Coworker plays the BIGOT role by saying, "I don't know what this place is coming to. We used to be a company of red, white, and blue Americans. Now we're being taken over by Japs and blacks!"	

Situation	Your Reaction/Role
Friend plays a DISHONEST role by saying, "Don't you work at Leo's Video Place? Any way you can sneak out some top videos for our party? I'd do it for you. After all, they'll think you're watching the videos to answer customers' questions."	
Coworker plays a PROVOCATIVE role by saying, "The way you get a raise around here is to wear hot clothes for the boss! That way you get more attention and a bigger paycheck!"	
Employer plays the PREJUDICED role by saying, "I read your resume and I know you have the right qualifications, but just one sign of any drug use and you're out the door, wheelchair and all! I'm not going to risk my company because of you."	

Job Success Skills

 ach situation in this section tests the skills that you may need to be successful in the world of work. Read each story and check the best response. Then discuss your choice with your instructors, parents, and friends to find out what they think the best response is.

Frayed Nerves

Gloria is an electronics repair technician at the NASA Space Center. The last two space flights went smoothly, but there's a lot of pressure on for the April launch. Scientists from other countries are going to be visiting the launch site, and the eyes of the world will be on the lift-off. Gloria is getting so tense that she keeps making careless mistakes with minor repairs. She has also been a little rude with her coworkers. What should she do?

___ Take tranquilizers to calm down.

___ Tell her supervisor that the pressure of the upcoming flight is too much for her.

___ Slow down her pace and ask a coworker to help check her work.

___ Accept that she's nervous and hope for calmer times.

You Gave Your Word!

Walter, vice president of a videotape distributing firm, wants to hire a new personnel manager. The present manager is finishing up a two-year contract but is incompetent, so Walter does not intend to renew that contract. Walter's likely choice for the job is Sam, the personnel manager's assistant. Sam has shown loyalty to the firm and competence in his work. Walter secretly tells Sam, "The position will be yours and your salary will be increased." Sam is delighted. Expecting the raise, Sam puts a down payment on a condominium for his family. Just one month later, the firm's president tells Walter that he has his own replacement for the personnel manager "waiting in the wings." The president said, "I've promised the job to Mr. Eager." What should Walter do?

___ Tell the president about his promise to Sam.

___ Avoid the whole issue and let a formal office memo tell Sam the bad news.

___ Apologize to Sam and say, "The hiring was taken out of my hands."

___ Look for another department where Sam could get a promotion.

Misplaced Authority

The Hyrise Corporation, an educational publishing firm, just hired a new editorial supervisor. Ms. Jacobs came highly recommended with a background in journalism and copyediting. But she doesn't have any experience in education and has never spent a day teaching. Within a month, Ms. Jacobs is criticizing the math writing team that's developing a textbook for students with special learning needs. Tempers flare. The math writers resent Ms. Jacobs' orders. What does she know about teaching math to disabled kids? Ms. Jacobs throws her weight around and demands that the book be written her way. What should the math writers do?

____ Tell Ms. Jacobs off!

____ Do it her way, because she is their supervisor.

____ Meet with Ms. Jacobs to express their concerns and show why their way is good.

____ Start a petition to get Ms. Jacobs fired.

Covering for Your Business Partner

Five years ago three heart doctors — cardiologists — formed a partnership. Because they all graduated from the same medical school, they seemed to have the same goals and interests. The partnership has been successful and has built an excellent reputation. But one problem has begun to surface. Dr. Santana, 42 years old and recently divorced, has begun to have problems with alcohol. The pressures of his job and the divorce have become unbearable. Patients are complaining to the other doctors that they can smell alcohol on Dr. Santana's breath, and that he doesn't seem to care when offering medical advice. Recently, he was unable to complete an operation. What should his two partners do?

____ Talk with Dr. Santana about the problem.

____ Hire a lawyer to remove Dr. Santana from the partnership.

____ Ask an Alcoholics Anonymous representative to secretly visit the office to judge how serious Dr. Santana's condition is.

____ Call his ex-wife and ask her to help.

Accepting Criticism

Mona has worked very hard in her new position as social director in the Valley Health Care Facility for senior citizens. Using skills from her clinical counseling background and research from her continuing education, she carefully plans an individual social program for each client. But her latest evaluation from her supervisor has given her a shock! Her ratings are much lower than she expected, and she's not getting even a small raise. Mona's supervisor says it's because the families of some patients complain that Mona "expects too much from their loved ones," and because coworkers say Mona has a "superior attitude." What should Mona do?

___ Look for another job.

___ Yell at the supervisor in anger.

___ Give up her special ideas and perform only her routine duties.

___ Explain to the supervisor why she works the way she does and how the clients benefit from her approach.

The Whistle Blower

Chris is a pilot for a small airline. After graduation from a leading flight school, Chris received his pilot's license and landed a job with the newest commuter service. But Chris is shocked by the work environment at flight headquarters. The mechanics seem very casual in preparing planes for flight. Some pilots arrive at the airport only minutes before takeoff. Important records, like flight logs, are handled carelessly. The traffic controllers sometimes permit dangerously low flights. Chris wants to be a superior pilot who flies safely and responsibly for an airline that does the same. What should he do?

___ Contact the Federal Aviation Administration anonymously.

___ Look for a job at an airline where safety standards are more strictly enforced.

___ Discuss his concerns with other pilots.

___ Ignore the problems and get used to them.

Facing Discrimination

Rose works for a paper distributing firm. She has been with the company for three years as a quality control supervisor. Ken holds the same position in another department. His duties and job description are identical to Rose's. Rose and Ken have both been with the company for three years. In fact, they were interviewed on the same day. A management position recently became available. Rose applied for the job, and so did Ken. Ken got it. When Rose asked why she didn't get the promotion, the company owner answered, "Rose, this job needs a man. People respect a male manager more. You understand, don't you?" What should Rose do?

___ Write to the U. S. Equal Opportunity Employment Commission to report a violation of her rights.

___ Spread gossip about Ken so his workers won't obey him.

___ Meet with the owner to discuss the issue of discrimination and her right to receive fair and equal treatment.

___ Write a letter to the local newspaper, exposing the owner's remarks.

Over Your Head

Mario was always a good student. He never worried about getting a good job because everyone just expected him to do well. In his first position, as an assistant to the sales manager at an auto dealership, Mario was an instant success. He was well groomed. He liked people and knew the right things to say. The supervisor wanted Mario to learn all there was to know about sales. He kept giving Mario information — marketing reports and sample sales agreements — to study on his own. Mario took all this help lightly, thinking he'd never need to know the information in those papers. He never really studied them. Last Tuesday, the supervisor suffered a heart attack. He was rushed to the hospital, and Mario suddenly had to handle six appointments with customers, including one very important customer who bought many cars for his business. Mario was totally unprepared. What should he do?

___ Fake his way through the appointments.

___ Reschedule them, hoping the supervisor will get better soon.

___ Ask a coworker (who hasn't really warmed up to Mario) to bail him out.

___ Try to learn more about the knowledge and skills needed by auto sales managers.

Pay Attention

Kate did it again! She forgot to save the computer file she was working on and lost a three-page report that her supervisor was expecting by noon. It was already 11:30. Kate hurriedly put her notes back together and started over. But she knew she couldn't make that deadline. She felt extra pressure because last week she accidentally left out three pages of a report for the executives. She thought she'd stop making mistakes if only she and her boyfriend would stop arguing. Then she'd be able to keep her mind on her work. But already, Kate's supervisor has had enough of her mistakes! What should Kate do?

___ Pretend to be sick, and take a day off to resolve her problems with Noah.

___ Promise "never to make a mistake again."

___ Blame her mistakes on interruptions from her coworkers.

___ Leave her personal problems at home when she comes to work.

Target of Envy

Nita worked as an administrative assistant at a community college. One thing Nita could be sure of was plenty of work to do. Sometimes she was almost too busy, but she enjoyed the challenge and was loyal to her boss. Lately, the other administrative assistants have been picking on Nita about how hard she works. While they're getting their morning coffee and chatting, Nita is at her desk, already into her day's work. Some coworkers are beginning to resent Nita. They feel she's making them look bad. To Nita's face, they pretend to worry that she's working too hard. They say they're concerned about her rights, but Nita knows how they really feel. What should she do?

___ Work a little slower to make peace with the others.

___ Keep doing her work the same way, because her boss depends on her.

___ Report the coworker's harassment to the college's worker relations committee.

___ Avoid her coworkers.

Working for Yourself

**S**tarting your own business is not a new idea. All through history, innovative, creative people have sought to do their best work by starting companies. These people could be called "self-starters" because they were willing to take risks to pursue their goals and turn their dreams into reality.

Consider these people, all of whom started small businesses that became giant corporations:

- Mary Kay (cosmetics)
- Edwin Land (Polaroid® cameras)
- Laura Ashley (fashion)
- Henry Ford (Ford cars)
- Ben Cohen and Jerry Greenfield (Ben & Jerry's® ice cream)
- Levi Strauss (Levi's® blue jeans)
- Frank Perdue (chicken)
- Jane Fonda (exercise videos)
- Ray Kroc (McDonald's® hamburgers)

What do they all have in common? Leadership, persistence, and hard work. They all had what it takes to organize, manage, and assume the risks of a business enterprise. They didn't just want to make a million in the lottery. They worked hard to achieve their goals.

In America, everyone is free to start a business, and a surprising number take advantage of that opportunity. Business starters — "entrepreneurs" — can be found in shopping malls, corporations, urban centers, and rural communities. Some entrepreneurs succeed, but many fail — usually because of mismanagement, a poorly thought-out business plan, or not enough money to get the business up and running.

To understand whether you should work for yourself, look at some of the typical characteristics of entrepreneurs. Some people think entrepreneurs are born with a talent for sales. But being born to sell doesn't always mean success. A knack for doing something must be backed up by "know-how" — knowing how to do it.

The family is an important influence for success. People who start companies are likely to come from families in which their parents or other relatives were also self-employed. In such families, young people learn about the business from their parents or relatives.

People who start their own businesses also have the attitude that they control their own lives. They don't depend on luck. Entrepreneurs believe that hard work, determination, and careful planning can make their businesses succeed. Often, entrepreneurs are risk takers. But they also know that starting out on your own is risky. To lower the risk, they spend plenty of time learning about the business they want to create.

Although a person of any age can start a business, most entrepreneurs are between 25 and 40 years old. Younger people often do start up new companies. But sometimes they have to delay their dreams while they pay back school loans or meet other obligations.

Before trying to start a business, think carefully about whether you really want to, and whether you have the right personality to work for yourself. Being your own boss means more work than a nine-to-five job. Any entrepreneur will tell you that if you aren't willing to work weekends, nights, and every day, then you're not likely to succeed. For young people starting families and also starting new businesses, trying to meet the responsibilities of both can be tough.

Many people say good health is part of the profile of an entrepreneur. Healthy self-esteem is also important, because how you feel about yourself affects how you feel about your work and how you relate to others. Customers and clients want to interact with people who are positive and comfortable with themselves. Starting your own business is really about selling yourself.

Successful entrepreneurs also develop their ability to communicate. Perhaps you learned about this **Hire Learning** skill in Book 1 when you explored your ability to get along with others, be a team player, and show sensitivity and tolerance for the ideas and feelings of others. You also learned how speaking, writing, listening, and body language affect relationships. All of these interpersonal skills are important for succeeding in your own business.

An entrepreneur has to be a salesperson, promoting the company's image, products, and services. You must pay special attention to your personal appearance, personal integrity, and professional know-how. Through these qualities, you will "package" yourself in a way that attracts customers and clients to your business. You'll need to use your business card to advertise, network, and make contacts.

Whether you plan to take over a family business, start a new company, or buy a franchise, you must first develop your "getting to know you" mentality. Entrepreneurship is like any career choice. Self-study is part of your education and training. It is the basis for decisions you'll make now and in the future.

Do I Have What It Takes?

any people dream of owning a successful business. They have different reasons:

- Freeing themselves from a nine-to-five daily work routine
- Being their own boss
- Doing what they want, when they want to do it
- Improving their standard of living
- Escaping unhappiness or boredom with their present job
- Enjoying the satisfaction of fulfilling a need for a product or service

Although some reasons are better than others, no reason is wrong. However, there are trade-offs you must make to start and run a business. That's where self-study becomes essential. Going into business requires certain personal characteristics. The next exercise is designed to help you discover whether you have the right characteristics to own and manage a business.

Read the following questions, and circle the letter beside the answer that says what you feel or comes closest to you. Be honest with yourself.

Are you a self-starter?

A I do things on my own. Nobody has to tell me to get going.

B If someone gets me started, I can keep going.

C Easy does it. I don't start until I have to.

How do you feel about other people?

A I like people. I can get along with just about anybody.

B I have plenty of friends — I don't need anyone else.

C Most people irritate me.

Can you lead others?

A I can get most people to go along with me.

B I can give the orders if someone tells me what we should do.

C I let someone else get things started. Then I go along if I feel like it.

Can you take responsibility?

A I like to take charge of things and see them through.

B I'll take over if I have to, but I'd rather let someone else take charge.

C Somebody always wants to show how smart he or she is by taking control — and I say they can have it!

How good an organizer are you?

A I like to have a plan before I start. I'm usually the one to get things lined up when the group wants to do something.

B I do all right unless things get too confused. Then I quit.

C I get all set and then something comes along and presents too many problems. So I just take things as they come.

How good a worker are you?

A I can keep going as long as I need to. I don't mind working hard for something I want.

B I'll work hard for a while but when I've had enough, that's it.

C I can't see that hard work gets you anywhere.

Can you make decisions?

A I can make up my mind in a hurry if I have to. It usually turns out okay too.

B I can if I have plenty of time. If I have to make up my mind fast, I feel unsure of myself.

C I don't like to be the one who has to decide things.

Can people trust what you say?

A You bet they can. I don't say things I don't mean.

B I try to be honest most of the time, but sometimes I just say what's easiest or what people want to hear.

C Why bother being truthful if the other person doesn't know the difference?

Can you stick with something you begin?

A If I make up my mind to do something, I don't let anything stop me.

B I usually finish what I start — if it goes well.

C If it doesn't go well from the start, I quit. Why beat your brains out?

How good is your health?

A I never run down!

B I have enough energy for most things I want to do.

C I run out of energy sooner than most of my friends seem to.

Now add up the letters you circled:

How many A's did you circle? ____

How many B's? ____

How many C's? ____

There were 10 questions in all. If you circled mostly A's, you probably have what it takes to run a business. If not, you may have more trouble than you can handle by yourself. Think about finding a partner who is strong in the ways that you're not. If you circled many C's, you may not be suited to starting a business — even with a partner.

As you continue to study yourself and consider your options, learn more about small businesses. You can contact the U. S. Small Business Administration (SBA) by calling 800-368-5855,

or contact your local SBA office. Other resources include state and local Small Business Development Centers, Economic Development Agencies, Chambers of Commerce, and professional organizations.

You'll also find information in bookstores and libraries. A useful book from JIST Works is *Mind Your Own Business: Getting Started as an Entrepreneur*, by LaVerne Ludden and Bonnie Maitlen.

Don't forget to rely on the voice of experience — friends or relatives who started their own businesses, college students majoring in business and management programs, and retired business people. Everything and everyone is there to help you.

A Business Opportunity in Your Future?

f you know you want to start a business, but don't know what kind of business, how do you start?

You want to make sure to choose a business that's needed where you live. You also want to make sure there isn't too much competition already. Finding a business that meets these requirements is called finding a "niche," just as different animals each find their own niche in nature.

You can use the library or a computerized career information system to identify the fastest growing occupations in your area. But that's only the beginning. You need to match your skills to market needs. If these don't make a comfortable match, you are heading down the road to failure.

You may be a performer who entertains at birthday parties or family gatherings. Already you've paved the way for a career in entertainment or as the owner of a party favors store — unless there are too many similar businesses already in your area. If you do have competition, should you abandon your idea to be a party planner? Not necessarily, but you need to think

of something that would make your service different from the others.

What's the key to success? Provide a product or service that is unique and in greater demand than the competition can serve. This type of thinking is called "market analysis," and it takes time and effort.

Suppose you want to start a new fast-food chain. You'll be competing with giants like McDonald's® and Wendy's®. You must research the current fast-food market to find out whether there's enough demand for fast food in your area to make room for another chain. You have to make sure that demand is growing, not shrinking, so your business can have a future. You also have to develop an idea for your restaurant that will pull people away from your competitors and draw them to you — lower prices, different menu, etc.

The Small Business Administration offers the following questions to help people analyze markets to determine whether a product or service will sell. If you have an idea, invention, product, or service you think may sell, and you have the personal traits of an entrepreneur, use these questions to help evaluate your plans.

	Yes	No	Comments
Do you know who your customers will be?	___	___	_____
Do you understand their needs and desires?	___	___	_____
Do you know where they live?	___	___	_____
Will you offer the kinds of products or services that they will buy?	___	___	_____
Will your prices be competitive in quality and value?	___	___	_____
Will your promotional program be effective?	___	___	_____
Do you understand how your business compares with your competitors?	___	___	_____
Will your business be conveniently located for the people you plan to serve?	___	___	_____
Will parking facilities be adequate for the people you plan to serve?	___	___	_____

"Small businesses range in size from a manufacturer with many employees and millions of dollars in equipment to the lone window washer with a bucket and sponge. Obviously, the knowledge and skills required for these two extremes are far apart, but, for success, they have one thing in common — each has found a business niche and is filling it."

—SBA Form 1414

Service with a Smile

 business can supply either a product or a service. Service businesses are often a good choice for an entrepreneur. Listed below are businesses that can be classified as services. You may already have provided many of these services for others, either as a volunteer or for pay.

Review the list and place a checkmark next to any service you have performed. Think of any other services you have performed, and add them to the appropriate category.

Arts and Crafts Services

____ Making jewelry

____ Stenciling

____ Designing wreaths

____ Demonstrating crafts

Landscape Services

____ Mowing lawns

____ Planting flowers

____ Raking and weeding

____ Watering gardens

Automotive Services

____ Washing cars

____ Cleaning car interiors

____ Changing tires

____ Changing oil and filter

Child Care

____ Caring for brothers and sisters

____ Helping with day care

____ Assisting with Head Start

____ Tutoring in reading and writing

Clerical Services

____ Answering the telephone

____ Acting as receptionist

____ Filing papers

____ Typing letters

Community Action

___ Working in political campaigns

___ Polling citizens

___ Conducting historical tours

Musical Services

___ Playing an instrument

___ Repairing instruments

___ Performing

___ Demonstrating equipment

Newspaper Distribution

___ Delivering papers

___ Collecting payments

___ Soliciting new customers

Personal Services

___ Housesitting

___ Catering

___ Nanny day care

___ Gift wrapping

Pet Care

___ Feeding animals

___ Exercising animals

___ Grooming animals

___ Training animals

Food Service

___ Serving customers

___ Stocking shelves

___ Bundling groceries

___ Working at farm stands

Health Care

___ Working in a hospital

___ Conducting social activities

___ Working in a hospital gift shop

___ Providing home health care

Home Improvement

___ Painting

___ Washing windows

___ Repairing and remodeling

___ Maintaining property

Repair and Maintenance

___ Repairing bicycles

___ Servicing autos

___ Repairing clocks

___ Working with tools

Retail Sales

___ Selling sportswear

___ Selling photo business cards

___ Participating in marketing internship

___ Telephone sales representative

Sport and Recreation Services

___ Umpiring

___ Collecting tickets

___ Reporting events

___ Organizing events

Starting Your Own Business

 ow's your chance to play the role of the entrepreneur. Design a new product that makes any of the services previously listed easier to perform, less expensive, or more available and competitive in the business world.

In the space provided, write as much as you can about your new product. Notice how much you need to decide about your new product before you can move forward with your plan.

_____

Service Category (from "Service with a Smile," page 72)

_____

Product Description

_____

Product Name (if you feel creative)

_____

Need for Product (be specific)

_____

Customer Identification (age, lifestyle, reason for needing product)

_____

Competition (other similar products)

_____

Unique Features (needs met by your product that will create customer demand)

_____

Raw Materials Needed

_____

Equipment / Machines Needed

Supplier(s) for Equipment / Production

_____

Length of Time to Produce

_____

Costs Associated with Design and Manufacture

_____

Safety Devices Required

_____

Test Market (people to try out product)

_____

Building / Product Location (space, parking, layout)

_____

Employees Needed (type and number)

_____

Capital (money needed for startup)

_____

Source of Capital (bank, investors, etc.)

Product Logo

Advertising (type, frequency, and message)

Celebrity Endorsement (optional)

Price of Product (compare with competitors)

Inventory (how much and how many products in stock)

Recordkeeping (method for recording sales, income, expenses)

Licenses / Permits / Business Laws to Be Followed

Protection (fire, theft, robbery, vandalism, accident liability insurance, and security)

Other Categories (as recommended by partners, instructors, mentors)

Showcase Your Product

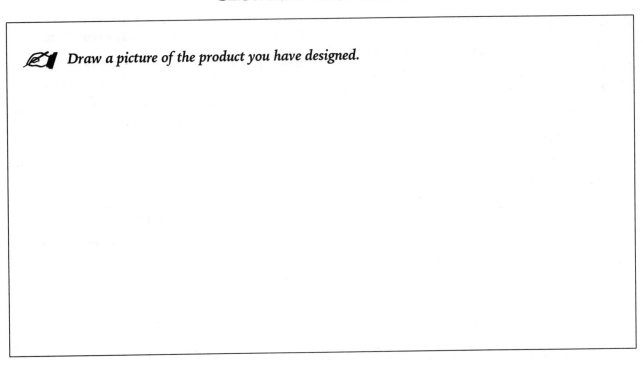

✍ *Draw a picture of the product you have designed.*

Advertise Your Product

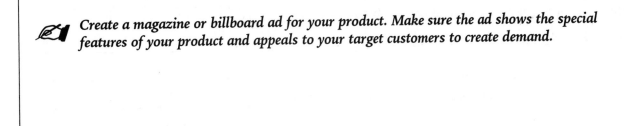

✍ *Create a magazine or billboard ad for your product. Make sure the ad shows the special features of your product and appeals to your target customers to create demand.*

Learning from the Experience of Others

Owning and running a business is a continuous learning process. Every entrepreneur has had similar experiences, yet each has learned from different resources: parents, teachers, mentors, courses, research, and most of all, practical experience.

To truly understand the world of the entrepreneur, you must meet one and ask the questions that will answer whether entrepreneurship is in your future. Use the questions below to conduct an information interview with someone who started a business.

Remember that some people start their career planning by working for someone else. Later on, they start their own businesses. Some people do both at the same time! In any case, the secret to success is planning ahead. Learn all there is to know, make some decisions . . . and then go out and learn some more.

Entrepreneur Information Interview Form

Interviewer: _____

Interviewee: _____

Business: _____

Address: _____

Day / date / time: _____

What is the nature of your business? _____

What types of products or services do you provide? _____

Why did you choose to become a small business owner? _____

_____

How long have you been operating your own business? _____

_____

Did you work for a corporation or company before starting your own business? If so, what type of work did you do and why did you decide to go into business for yourself?

_____

_____

How did you pick a name for your business? _____

_____

Where is your business located? Are you satisfied with your location? _____

_____

Entrepreneur Information Interview Form

What effect do you think location has on success? _____

_____

What are the greatest advantages in owning your own business? _____

_____

What drawbacks do you find in small business ownership? _____

_____

What types of products and services do you feel will be needed for the 21st century? _____

_____

What types of community services / agencies / workers can be of greatest assistance to a person just starting out?

_____

_____

If a young person wanted to start his or her own business, what advice would you give that person?

_____

_____

If a person owned a seasonal small business, how would you recommend that he or she spend the off season? Take another job, refurbish the property, create new products?

_____

_____

What types of skills are necessary for success in a small business? _____

_____

What are the most important types of interpersonal skills for a business owner? _____

_____

How does small business ownership affect a person's leisure time? _____

_____

Entrepreneur Information Interview Form

How have you advertised your business? What types of advertising have you found most successful and why?

_____

_____

What is your opinion of a business partnership? _____

_____

What qualities should a person consider when choosing a business partner? _____

_____

_____

What types of problems can arise in a business partnership? _____

_____

_____

For the problems you have mentioned, what solutions do you recommend? _____

_____

What situations should be avoided when operating a small business? _____

_____

How do the services of bankers, attorneys, and manufacturers affect the small business owner?

_____

_____

How does the national or global economy affect the small business owner? _____

_____

How does the state or federal government affect the small business owner? _____

_____

If you were going to hire employees to work for you and represent your business, what personal qualities, values, and skills would you seek in applicants?

_____

_____

Making a Job Change

People change. Jobs change. People change jobs.

These statements reveal today's fast-paced world of work. People change jobs and careers frequently. It is estimated that most people will make at least three major career switches, and eight to ten different job changes, in their lifetimes.

Life used to be a lot simpler. Most workers remained in the same position, or with the same company, until retirement. They got an occasional promotion or shift in responsibility, but more often they faced boredom, stress, and burnout.

Work today is vastly different. There are many trends affecting the job market that will continue into the 21st century. Consider some of these trends:

- Technology is changing work environments. In particular, the computer is influencing every career. It is altering tasks and creating a demand for trained workers who can adapt and adjust to the information explosion. Computer skills are a necessity for all workers.
- Large numbers of new immigrants are entering the workforce, sometimes with high skill levels and strong determination to succeed. Some U.S.-born workers may have to relocate or retrain in order to compete.
- Women appear in the workforce and the political arena in increasing numbers. Many women are seeking influential positions in fields that previously were not open to them. Although barriers still exist in high-level positions, women are looking beyond that "glass ceiling" and being taken seriously in the business world.
- Medical technology has created new occupations. Ethical issues related to health care have blended medical careers with law, economics, and governmental studies.

- Minorities are entering the workforce in record numbers. African Americans, Hispanics, Asian Americans, Native Americans, and other ethnic groups have created a multicultural employee mix. Bilingual workers will be highly valued in this environment.

- Small business is on the rise. Entrepreneurs are starting their own businesses, often leaving the corporate world to work for themselves. They are willing to put in long hours and learn new skills to take advantage of new opportunities. Minority-owned and woman-owned businesses are a growing segment of entrepreneurship.

- People are living longer. This is adding several new twists to the job market: an increased need for geriatric occupational services, competition for employment between elders and young workers, and career changes at an age that used to be considered time to retire.

- People are trying harder to find a balance in their lifestyles. Men and women want to have more time for their families and for community, social, and leisure activities. Climbing the ladder of success at the expense of home and family is not viewed as healthy or desirable. This new perspective has resulted in programs like job sharing, flex time, and new part-time options.

- Some work tasks are still performed independently, but there is a growing emphasis on joint decision making and teamwork.

- Schools are doing more to help students make the transition from school to work. Role models, mentors, tutors, and education/business partnerships are striving to help students finish school and find employment after graduation.

- Some students are enrolled in community colleges while still in high school. This transition program encourages continuing education, resulting in better employment opportunities for young people and a more skilled workforce.

- More people are choosing to work at home in "home offices." Many use phones, fax machines, and computers to link up with the larger companies for which they work.

In addition to the effects of these trends, other reasons why people change jobs are:

Physical and mental health
Better location
Opportunity or desire for further education
Opportunity to meet career and life goals
Inadequate working conditions
Overqualified for the position
Family responsibilities
Need time and energy for personal interests
Desire for more challenging work
Job stress level
Unavailability of position for which trained
Seeking a promotion, advancement, and recognition for achievements
Change in local, national, or global economy and demand for services or products
Seeking better benefits (for self and/or family)
Job ceases to exist (company sold, shut down, merger, etc.)
Desire for greater personal growth
Need for greater job security
Relationships with supervisors, coworkers
Discriminatory attitudes and actions

The most basic job changes are getting fired, getting promoted, and quitting. **Hire Learning** covers each of these in this section. No matter what the reason for change, the important thing to remember is to make the change properly. If you don't handle your exit from a job carefully, you may hurt your chances for jobs in the future.

On the Firing Line

It would be nice to think that once you land a job, your troubles are over. Nice — but not very realistic. Things do go wrong. However, what matters is how you handle yourself when things go wrong.

You can get fired for several reasons. Most reasons are problems you can prevent — if you are aware of how negative attitudes, negative behavior, and inadequate job performance affect employers, supervisors, and coworkers.

Most often, job problems happen not because a worker lacks skill, but because of the worker's attitudes, behavior, and relationships with others. When problems come up, each workplace has its own set of steps for dealing with them. Some employers are more lenient than others, but they usually take several steps before firing a worker: a verbal warning, an official written warning, suspension (for a period of time), and then dismissal (firing).

Keep in mind that problems in the workplace are not one-sided. Sometimes, an angry employee isn't willing to take the blame for excessive lateness or absence, or for showing a negative attitude when given orders. The employee may complain about being hassled or picked on. But the employer has a responsibility to run the business efficiently. When workers don't perform well, or when they bring personal problems into the workplace, the company has to take action. Problems like clumsiness, wastefulness, or friction with coworkers all affect a worker's job performance. Companies have deadlines to meet, products to manufacture, and services to provide. They can only do these tasks with workers who are efficient and cooperative. A company does not want to fire people — after all, bosses are people too and usually don't enjoy firing anybody. Too much firing gives a company a bad name, and when people are fired, it's costly to find and train replacements.

To avoid firing, companies try to help their workers stay productive. They may offer Employee Assistance Programs (EAP) to help with problems that may affect job performance, or they may offer programs that make doing a good job rewarding for workers. Such programs may include:

- Alcoholics Anonymous meetings for workers
- Health and fitness programs
- Substance abuse counseling and rehabilitative services
- Day care facilities and programs for employees with young children and aging parents
- Flexible hours
- Foreign language policies and cultural celebrations
- Sabbaticals (leaves) for continuing education
- Profit sharing plans
- Quality circles to encourage involvement and team planning
- Training programs for leadership and management positions

Beyond such programs, all employers have job performance standards. In every job you take, you must be careful to build up a good work record. Frequent absences, tardiness, and hopping from one job to another all point to a person who may not be reliable. If you follow the rules, learn company policies, put forth your best effort, show initiative, and always give a little more than what is expected, chances are you'll be a valued employee.

In addition to showing a positive attitude and responsible behavior, you need to perform well in basic reading, writing, listening, speaking, and math tasks. Math mistakes cost a company money. Mistakes in spelling, grammar, and punctuation hurt your image. If you can't follow oral and written directions accurately, you'll annoy your supervisor and also bring closer supervision on yourself. Asking reasonable questions about procedures you don't understand is acceptable, but frequent questioning about simple tasks becomes irritating. An employer could easily conclude that you aren't interested in putting forth your best effort, or that you just aren't capable of performing the assigned task.

Although poor basic skills can get you warned or fired, evidence of attitude problems causes the greatest concern for employers. Inappropriate clothing, sulking when corrected or criticized, extending breaks, using drugs or alcohol at work or before work, making phony excuses for being late, or not showing up at work can seriously affect how long you keep a job. No matter what type of work you are doing, be positive, show effort, and be honest, mature, and enthusiastic. That's how you keep a job.

Many successful chairpersons of large corporations, as well as owners of small businesses, offer similar advice to those entering any job or career position:

✓ **Work hard and don't watch the clock.**

✓ **Learn to listen to anyone and everyone.**

✓ **Learn to get along with others.**

✓ **Value personal integrity and be proud of yourself.**

✓ **Be a team player.**

✓ **Be tolerant of differing values, cultures, and points of view.**

✓ **Take advantage of opportunities to learn and grow.**

Remember, attitude determines altitude. Follow this **Hire Learning** advice, and you probably won't end up on the firing line.

Are You Promotable?

ost people think a promotion is something you get only after a long time in a position. But advancing toward a possible promotion is a goal you should seek from the first day you get a job. Making a good impression and showing initiative and responsible behavior from your first day can add up over weeks, months, and years to advancement opportunities.

Of course, it's unreasonable to expect a pay raise or promotion after only a brief time on the job (unless a quick raise was promised to you when you were hired). Most employers have a three to six month probationary period for new employees before any raise or promotion is possible. After that, if a worker's performance has been very good, a promotion is possible, along with a raise and increased responsibilities. These rewards can also include further education at the company's expense or increased benefits. Employee unions and professional organizations within a workplace usually have guidelines and procedures to assure that all workers are given equal opportunity for advancement.

How Not to Get Promoted

Certain attitudes and behaviors can cut your chances for promotion. These are not always written in the employee handbook, and they may not be obvious, like taking drugs or making long personal phone calls at work. Some promotion-killing behaviors include:

✓ **Aggressive or "know-it-all" attitude.**

There is a place and time to be aggressive, but pushing too hard, too often, annoys employers and coworkers. Showing off your superiority and putting others down makes work unpleasant and destroys morale. No employer needs you if you think you are better than the rest of the world.

✓ **Expecting to be number one.**

There are plenty of talented, able people out there. Doing a good job doesn't automatically entitle you to a raise or promotion over someone else.

✓ **Complaining and pointing out the faults and failings of others.**

No one gives you the right to criticize others or complain about their mistakes or inadequacies. A complainer brings everyone down. If you think you're impressing the boss by tattling on others or pointing out their weaknesses, think again. That strategy will backfire.

✓ Becoming too friendly with your supervisor.

Even though a company may have a friendly atmosphere, you shouldn't try to become a pal of your boss or supervisor. Also refrain from any romantic involvement with supervisors or coworkers.

✓ Threatening to leave or work for a competitor.

This type of threat may seem appropriate if you feel unappreciated in your present job. But no one likes a threat. If you threaten to leave, your boss will probably open the door and tell you to go ahead. You can forget changing your mind — the damage will be done. If you don't follow through and quit, you'll probably be fired anyway.

Can you think of other examples of behavior that could hurt your chances for promotion? Discuss these examples with your instructors and offer alternatives and examples of better behavior.

 pportunities for promotion and advancement can come in different ways:

- Another worker quits or gets fired, so his or her job becomes available.
- Another worker is promoted.
- You demonstrate superior performance and are rewarded with a better paying position.
- A new position is created.
- A new branch office or department is opened and needs workers to move up from other parts of the company.

Planning for advancement is a personal process. Advancement means more than additional pay. It means personal recognition and greater responsibilities. You should discuss your plans with those who would be affected by change in your work, such as parents, your spouse, or other family members.

If you want to be promoted, you have to evaluate your present performance to make sure you're doing your best. Review the following chart. For each statement, check whether your performance in that area is *very good, adequate, needs improvement* or whether that statement *doesn't apply* to you. Be ready to give examples to back up your answers.

Remember, promotions are earned. They require positive behaviors and effort beyond the normal expectations of the job. But realize too that some people do not want to be promoted. They like it just where they are.

My Promotion Quotient	Very Good	Adequate	Needs Improvement	Doesn't Apply
If my supervisor or employer were evaluating me, how would he or she rate my job performance?	_____	_____	_____	_____
The amount and quality of work I do, compared with my coworkers	_____	_____	_____	_____
The number of mistakes I make on the job	_____	_____	_____	_____
The number of times I repeat the same mistake	_____	_____	_____	_____
My loyalty to the company/organization	_____	_____	_____	_____
My punctuality (am I on time?)	_____	_____	_____	_____
My attendance record (am I absent much?)	_____	_____	_____	_____
My knowledge of company rules and regulations	_____	_____	_____	_____
My interest in and attitude toward my work	_____	_____	_____	_____
My ability to get along with others	_____	_____	_____	_____
My respect for myself and for those I work with	_____	_____	_____	_____
My ability to meet deadlines and react calmly in a crisis	_____	_____	_____	_____
My ability to accept criticism and improve myself based on what is expected of me	_____	_____	_____	_____
My ability to show initiative and resourcefulness	_____	_____	_____	_____
My desire for self-improvement	_____	_____	_____	_____
My care with company supplies and equipment	_____	_____	_____	_____
My tolerance for ideas, values, and beliefs different from my own	_____	_____	_____	_____
My ability to adapt to changes in my duties and technological advances	_____	_____	_____	_____

Valued Employee

 ation's Business recently featured an article by Sharon Nelton that truly reflected the practices valued in **Hire Learning**. The entire article was devoted to motivating workers through praise and recognition. In the article, businesses from across the country told of increased worker self-esteem, greater productivity and loyalty, and an absence of laziness. This came about because bosses made an effort to recognize their employees by "saying thank you, writing notes when workers have done a good job, honoring them with awards, praising them publicly, and being honest, sincere, and fair."

Why praise workers? Everyone likes to feel appreciated and to know that the quality of his or her work is valued. Praise is one of the basic needs and wants of human beings. Often the best employees are those who have been recognized for their good work.

Pretend that you are employed. You have been trying to put into practice the **Hire Learning** behaviors introduced in this school-to-work transition program. In what way would you like to be recognized? In the space below, design a plaque, certificate, or incentive that would motivate you to be the best employee that you can be.

With Appreciation and Thanks

Resigning from a Job

veryone has known someone who looks forward to Friday when Monday's work has just begun. The relief that Friday has arrived quickly changes as Sunday night rolls around. Then depression sets in. This way of thinking shows that the person's work is not fulfilling or satisfying. But why? There are many possible reasons, including:

- A poorly made job or career decision
- A bad work environment
- Inability to get along with supervisors and coworkers
- A low-paying position with little chance of improvement
- Following someone else's career plan rather than choosing work that complements interests, talents, and abilities

There are usually signs along the way that show you should consider quitting — and not all of them are negative. Some good reasons for quitting are:

- To continue or update your education and training
- To accept a better paying job or position
- To relocate based on short- and long-term goals

Workers who think of quitting should first carefully examine their situations by asking themselves these questions:

Why do I want to quit?

Is the work unsatisfying, or have my attitudes and behaviors made it that way?

Can I cope with unemployment (loss of pay and benefits)?

Will I have to learn new skills to get another job?

Am I mentally, physically, and financially able to update my skills or continue my education?

Can I be sure that the problems in my present job won't come up in my next job, too?

What effect will quitting have on my work history and resume?

Will another position have the good points of my present job?

How do I usually react to changes in my personal life or work?

Have I checked out other options by reviewing my skills, abilities, aptitudes, and interests?

Can I describe to myself or someone else what truly motivates me — what work I would really LOVE to do?

Remember that just because job and career changes are common today, they don't have to be sudden or drastic. Some people prefer the security and stability of a long-term job or career choice.

If, after careful thought, you decide to quit, be careful to follow these pointers for making a graceful exit:

✓ **Inform your supervisor first.**

It is inconsiderate to allow your immediate supervisor to learn of your resignation plans second-hand.

✓ **Give enough notice.**

Submit your resignation in a letter long before your final day. The proper amount of notice (usually two weeks or a month) is a matter of company policy.

✓ **Give a tactful, professional reason for leaving.**

Good reasons include moving to a job with more personal growth opportunity or continuing your education. A positive but honest reason is better than a list of complaints, anger, or no reason at all. Remember that how gracefully you leave a job can affect your ability to get another job down the road.

✓ **Finish any unfinished duties.**

This leaves a positive impression of you as you leave. Your work station or office should be cleaned up and your personal belongings removed so that a new employee can move in.

✓ **Participate positively in any exit interview.**

If you're leaving on good terms, you probably have insights into your work experience and will want to share these thoughts in the exit interview. Leave a forwarding address or telephone number where you can be reached.

✓ **Don't play your hand too soon.**

Do not say anything about quitting — in writing or verbally — if you're waiting to be offered the job you're quitting for. When you do get an offer, do not use it to pressure your present or future employer to serve your own needs. Such behavior only works against you. Besides, if you have carefully considered a job change, you should have been investigating other options long before you make an actual move.

✓ **Study the official termination policies and procedures.**

That way you will know how the company expects you to behave and can conduct yourself in a professional manner.

✓ **Leave your present job with a positive attitude.**

Say goodbye to those you worked with. Don't hold grudges or badmouth anyone; such actions don't leave a favorable impression with your coworkers or supervisors.

✓ **Take time to personally say goodbye to your supervisor.**

The exit interview is an appropriate time to do this. If you have been a valued employee, you may want to ask the supervisor's permission to use his or her name as a reference when conducting future job searches.

Every job termination — whether a firing, promotion, or resignation — is different. Remember your **Hire Learning** behavior: A positive attitude and an honest approach to all personal and work situations is always the best policy.

The Exit Interview

nytime someone leaves a job, there's an opportunity for both the worker and the employer to learn and grow from that experience. An exit interview, if conducted properly by both sides, is an excellent way to accomplish this mutual growth.

Before exploring the sample exit interview on page 93, you need to learn about the types of job changes. Some of the most common include:

Lateral movement. The worker changes to a different job at basically the same level (no promotion) within the same company.

Promotion. The worker gets a new title, and sometimes better pay and fringe benefits, more authority, and more responsibility.

Transfer. The worker moves to a different location within the same company.

Resignation. The worker leaves the company voluntarily.

Retirement. The worker leaves voluntarily to begin collecting retirement benefits.

Termination. The worker is forced to leave the company.

An exit interview is a final interview between the employer and employee when the employee is leaving or changing jobs within the company. The interview is meant to find out about:

- The worker's reason(s) for leaving
- Changes the worker may wish to suggest to the company
- The worker's opinion of conditions and policies within the workplace
- Complaints the employee may have that can avoid lawsuits over such things as sexual harassment or discrimination

An exit interview is not always negative or confrontational. Sometimes people leave companies they like, to pursue further education or for other reasons. The employer-employee relationship may have been positive and rewarding. In those situations, an exit interview is as important as it is in those where conflict and dissatisfaction may have been a major cause for the job change.

Knowing the advantages and disadvantages of the interview — for employer and employee — helps both prepare for the interview.

Employer	Employee
Advantages	**Advantages**
Documentation of employee's reasons for leaving, which can be used in future referrals.	Opportunity to communicate satisfaction or dissatisfaction with the job.
Record of employment to evaluate for future rehiring.	Reinforces worker's self-esteem to feel opinions are valued by employer.
Input into possible changes of policies and practices that could benefit the company.	Gives sense of closure to this phase of his or her career life.
	Opportunity to discuss any biases or discriminatory actions or policies.
Disadvantages	
Hurt feelings if change is because of negative or confrontational issues.	**Disadvantages**
Waste of time if employee does not take interview seriously.	Fear of reprisal for negative comments.
	Possible waste of time if his or her ideas are never used.
Suggestions offered by employee may be unworkable or inappropriate.	Threat to self-esteem if employer reacts negatively to employee's ideas.

Not all companies include an exit interview as part of their policies and procedures. Sometimes, a letter of resignation is all that is required. However, an employee has a right to request an exit interview.

In companies that have the exit interview, different people can conduct the interview. Sometimes it's the worker's immediate supervisor, but other times it's a personnel officer. Each approach has its strengths and drawbacks.

The difference could be compared to a student's feelings about a grade in a course. The student must decide whether it's better to discuss the grade with the course instructor or speak to the head of the department. If there is a personality conflict between an instructor and a student, is it better to discuss the problem with the principal and a counselor or should the problem be addressed with the instructor?

Whatever you and your employer decide, use exit interviews as a way to grow.

Sample Exit
Interview

T he following questions are often asked by employers in exit interviews. While some may seem simplistic (such as the type of work that you do), they are included when the interview is conducted by someone other than an immediate supervisor. Naturally, in addition to the questions below, there would be job-specific questions about work tasks and responsibilities performed by an employee.

As in any interview, the employee should have carefully considered the comments that he or she wants to make before the interview begins. To prepare, it's a good idea to try a practice interview before the real thing. Gossip should not be a part of the interview. Only the facts should be up for discussion. If the worker is leaving for negative reasons and there is evidence in writing of the problems he or she faced, having these memos or other papers handy may be helpful.

Exit Interview Form

What was your position in this company? _____

How long were you employed with the company? _____

Did you have any other positions with this company? _____

Did you apply for and/or receive any promotions within the company? _____

_____

Do you feel you were discriminated against with any promotion? If so, why? _____

_____

What reasons do you see for your getting or not getting any promotions? _____

_____

Did you ever follow up with the appropriate supervisors as to why you did not qualify for a promotion? If so, what information were you looking for?

_____

_____

Do you feel you were ever discriminated against? Please explain. _____

_____

Exit Interview Form

What type of training did you have for your present position? _____
_____

Do you feel you were underqualified or overqualified for your job? Please explain. _____
_____

Did you enjoy your job? _____

Did you ever make any suggestions to management for changes in your job? If so, how were these suggestions received?

_____

_____

Do you feel management was responsive to your suggestions? _____
_____

What has satisfied you the most about your work? _____
_____

_____

What frustrations have you encountered with the job? _____
_____

_____

Do you feel you need continuing education to remain qualified for your job? _____
_____

Do you have any other suggestions for the company? _____
_____

_____

Like information interviews and job interviews, an exit interview has guidelines for appropriate and inappropriate responses and behaviors. Here are some examples of how to handle — or how not to handle — common exit interview questions.

Question: What was your position with the company?

Inappropriate response: "Well, you hired me as a short-order chef. But as you kept piling on the work, it seemed that I had to do everything that no one else wanted to do!"

Analysis: This type of remark sets up confrontation almost on the first question. It's negative and sounds as if it is coming from a complainer.

Question: How long were you with the company?

Inappropriate response: "Too long, that's why I'm quitting! There's too much stress here!"

Analysis: Again, the response is confrontational.

Question: Did you apply for any promotions within the company?

Appropriate response: "I applied for the position of executive secretary to the vice president."

Inappropriate response: "The pay here is lousy, so a promotion would have helped. But I soon found out that unless you're friends with the right people, you don't get ahead here."

Analysis: The inappropriate response is gossip and it's negative.

Question: Do you feel that you were discriminated against by this company?

Inappropriate response: "Absolutely! If you aren't Hispanic you can't make it here. Guess you guys want to make yourselves look good by hiring minorities, but I felt that as a white woman, I had to take a back seat to your cultural diversity hype. Then when Marguerita got supervisor over me when I had been here longer, I decided to quit!"

Analysis: This type of remark is off base in an interview. If there is documented evidence that company policy ties promotions to seniority, it is appropriate to bring that to the attention of the interviewer. Otherwise, the comments above are negative and don't serve any purpose.

Question: Do you feel that you were properly trained for your job?

Appropriate response: "Yes, when I first came to work for this company the supervisors were very helpful. They helped anyone who had difficulty and really took a personal interest in each of their employees. I also appreciate the opportunities that you gave me to learn on the job. As I said previously, my financial status did not let me go back to school immediately, so your support was most helpful."

Analysis: You can tell by this response that the employee is sincere and, as such, will be listened to with an open mind by the interviewer.

Question: What has satisfied you the most about your work?

Appropriate response: "I felt that the work I did on the medical research project would truly benefit society. Even though I was only one part of the project, I felt that my part was important. I also enjoyed the people I worked with, and that is why I often spent extra time on lab assignments and technical reports. I even found that some of my coworkers became my friends outside the workplace. It has been a good work environment, and I hope that I will be treated with as much respect in my next position."

Analysis: The interactions of people in any work site are vital to satisfaction and fulfillment, and in this response that is obvious. What type of work you do matters little as long as you feel respected by your supervisors and coworkers.

Learning
in the
Community

Throughout your **Hire Learning** experience you have heard instructors describe the classroom as your workplace. Your homework is like any real work task. Being on time is a work behavior valued in school and in employment. Getting along with others is important in both settings. So are sensitivity and tolerance for the thoughts, beliefs, and feelings of others. Your schoolwork has been linked to possible job and career choices, and you've learned how to gain new skills and experience in the community, the workplace of your future.

This chapter of **Hire Learning** offers some more ways to learn from community-based studies and experiences. Keep in mind that learning is a lifelong process. It does not take place just in a classroom, or even just in a workplace. By studying in the community, you will link what you have learned in school with skills that make you a valued worker and citizen.

Your instructors have led activities to help you better understand working. They have helped you identify jobs you may be interested in. By now, you may have taken field trips to work sites and watched workers in their day-to-day activities. Some of you may have been involved in cooperative vocational education programs that combine classroom instruction with on-the-job training. All of this experience has prepared you for entry-level jobs, apprenticeships, and internships.

More and more schools offer community-related programs to help build a more highly skilled workforce. If you have not looked into these programs in your school, ask your instructors or counselors about what your school offers.

Think about the subjects you enjoy the most or do well in. Then plan to take part in an independent study project or work/study program that applies your skills and aptitudes to a community project. Learn more about internships, apprenticeships, dual enrollment, and 2 + 2 tech-prep programs. There may be a summer program in which you could explore computer applications and systems with professionals from local government, universities, and companies. If the arts interest you, look into community programs that welcome young people to take part in theater, museum, and cultural activities. Whatever you like, get out there, get involved, and keep learning!

Most community-based programs that offer career preparation activities will ask you to:

- Keep a daily log or diary of what you've learned.
- Attend an orientation session.
- Design and present a special project based on what you've learned.
- Keep up with your schoolwork and grades during the program.
- Maintain a good attendance record in the program.
- Make a personal evaluation of your learning experience.
- Undergo an evaluation of your performance in the program.

The remaining pages offer forms on which you can record and evaluate your studies in the community. If you use these forms, be sure to transfer important information from them to your work history and resumé.

Internship Journal

T he purpose of the "internship journal" is to record what you experience and learn while at the job site during an internship, apprenticeship, cooperative vocational program, work/study program, or similar activity. The journal also helps you examine your physical, mental, and emotional readiness for a work environment.

Your internship journal should include information about you and the organization where you are interning. In addition it should include a daily diary of your observations, feeling, and experiences. Every day of your internship or other study program, note the date and describe what you did, what you learned, and how you felt about it. This information may be valuable for preparing or revising your work history and resumé.

The form below gives an example of the type of information your journal might include for each internship experience.

Internship Information Form

Name: _____

Address: _____

Telephone: _____

School: _____

Grade Level: _____

Homeroom Teacher: _____

Internship Coordinator: _____

Community Sponsor: _____

Organization / Company: _____

Address: _____

Telephone: _____

Beginning Internship Date: _____

Date	Activity

Which Skills Do I Have?
Which Do I Need?

All careers relate directly to education. All careers also have their own vocabulary. Think carefully about the work tasks you have performed during your internship. Then fill out this chart, which shows the relationship between education and work skills. Include your feelings about how well you performed each task. Discuss this part of the journal with your advisor or community sponsor to help evaluate your performance.

WORK TASK PERFORMED	SKILLS NEEDED			HOW WELL PERFORMED		
	Communication	Math	Specialized	Performed Satisfactorily	Improved Throughout Internship	Had Difficulty with Task

All in a Day's Work

T he questions below will help you evaluate your internship experience. Because each community work site provides different goods and services, and each has a different number of employees, some questions may not apply to your program. Read all the questions first. Then record your answers as you progress through your internship. You should schedule a meeting to discuss this journal with your internship sponsors. Be sure to complete all journal entries at the end of the internship.

Describe the work performed by the company or individual you're working for.

What skills and/or special training are required of workers at your internship site?

Are you taking any school courses that are required for this internship? If not, where can you go to increase your knowledge and skills for this job?

What responsibilities have been required of you at this work site?

Did your internship work site provide a service?

Did your internship work site manufacture a product? Yes / No (Explain).

Did your internship work site sell a product or service? Yes / No (Explain).

What kinds of equipment and tools are most frequently used by workers at the site?

What tools or equipment did you learn to use during the internship?

One way to match yourself with a suitable job is to compare the job with things you enjoy doing or would like to learn. Most jobs are about working with things, information, or people. Give examples of how you worked with each during your internship.

_____

Working with Things

_____

Working with Information

_____

Working with People

_____

Which category (things, information, people) do you work best with? Why?

 very job presents situations that relate to your personal, social, and work values. Examples of values in each of these areas could include:

PERSONAL

Self-worth
Leadership
Recognition
Loyalty
Knowledge
Belonging

SOCIAL

Human rights
Equal opportunity
Group rights
Teamwork
Respect for abilities
Willingness to adapt

WORK

Job security
Fair wages
Benefits
Competition
Advancement
Creativity

As you progress through your internship, think about the personal, social, and work values that were a part of your internship. Record your thoughts about each category.

_____

PERSONAL VALUES

Describe opportunities for leadership and recognition of a job well done at the work site.

As an intern, how were you greeted and introduced to the work and to people?

SOCIAL VALUES

Did your work site provide an environment where workers were involved in decisions about the company image, productivity, or worker rights?

What observations can you record about the "team spirit" at your work site?

WORK VALUES

What benefits are available to employees at your work site?

What promotion opportunities are available?

How are new employees trained when they enter this company?

Are you still interested in this job/career since you've had a chance to observe it first-hand? Why? Why not?

If your internship sponsor chose to hire you, would you accept the job? Why? Why not?

Which aspects of the internship did you find most enjoyable, educational, or challenging?

Enjoyable	*Educational*	*Challenging*

What did you find boring, difficult, or stressful?

Boring	*Difficult*	*Stressful*

What suggestions would you offer to improve school-to-work community activities?

Internship Self-Evaluation

On the chart below, describe your performance in each of the *internship experience* points listed. Use checkmarks to indicate whether the item applied to your experience *frequently, sometimes,* or *seldom.* Add any comments that describe your performance or can lead to improvement.

Name: _____

Grade/Age: _____

Career Interest: _____

School: _____

Teacher/Counselor: _____

Work Site: _____

Internship Experience	Frequently	Sometimes	Seldom	Comments
Participated in work tasks that were interesting				
Was given enough direction to do work tasks correctly				
Participated in a variety of work tasks				
Did things myself rather than just observing				
Discussed my work experiences with my instructors				
Discussed my work experiences with my parents and friends				
Felt that my effort was appreciated at the work site				
Felt I was treated fairly and as if I were a real employee				
Received help with work tasks when I was unsure of expectations				
Was able to apply things learned in school to this work experience				
Was helped to focus on my own future goals through this experience				

Community Sponsor
Evaluation

Here is a chart that lets you rate yourself from the viewpoint of your community sponsor. How would they judge your personal qualities and work performance? Use checkmarks to show how you performed the work tasks, from *excellent* to *poor,* or check that the item is *not applicable* to you or your internship. Add any comments that describe your performance or can lead to improvement. Use this exercise as a reminder of the types of personal qualities and work performance that your future work may require.

Intern: _____

Grade/Age: _____

School: _____

Career/Interest: _____

Length of Participation: _____

Instructor/Counselor: _____

Work Site: _____

Evaluator: _____

Telephone: _____

Personal Qualities / Work Performance	Excellent	Above Average	Average	Below Average	Poor	Not Applicable	Comments
Was friendly and cooperative							
Was accepted positively by other employees							
Was able to follow oral and written directions in doing tasks							
Reported to work site on time							
Was cooperative and industrious							
Was reliable and dependable							
Showed initiative and sought help (if needed)							
Acted maturely							
Exercised good judgment							
Was trustworthy and honorable							
Was neat and accurate in work tasks performed							
Was able to adapt to change (as it occurred) at the work site							
Wanted to learn							
Took pride in personal accomplishments							

Suggestions / Recommendations for Future School-to-Work Transition Programs:

Notes